MW01615367

Tao Calligraphy to Heal and Transform Depression and Anxiety

Tao Calligraphy to Heal and Transform Depression and Anxiety

Dr. & Master Zhi Gang Sha
#1 *NEW YORK TIMES* BESTSELLING AUTHOR

Praise for Dr. and Master Sha

"The universe is not made of matter; it is made of information. Information that is aligned with the structure of the universe heals. The Dao Calligraphy of Master Sha is evidently aligned with the structure of the universe—it heals. Dr. and Master Sha is a true messenger and Grandmaster of Dao."
— Dr. Ervin Laszlo
Founder of the Club of Budapest and
the Laszlo Institute of New Paradigm Research

"We, the human race, need more Zhi Gang Sha."
— Dr. Maya Angelou
author of *I Know Why the Caged Bird Sings*

"Practical, useful information and techniques for putting the body's natural abilities to work on healing —a wonderful contribution."
— Dr. Wayne Dyer
author of *Wishes Fulfilled: Mastering the Art of Manifesting*

"Dr. Sha is an important teacher and a wonderful healer with a valuable message about the power of the soul to influence and transform all life."
— Dr. Masaru Emoto
author of *The Hidden Messages in Water*

"Dr. Sha offers a clear, practical path to learning the secrets of self-healing."
— Marianne Williamson
author of *A Return to Love: Reflections on the Principles of A Course on Miracles*

"Dr. Sha's techniques awaken the healing power already present in all of us, empowering us to put our overall well-being in our own hands. His explanation of energy and message, and how they link consciousness, mind, body, and spirit, forms a dynamic information network in language that is easy to understand and, more important, to apply."
— Michael Bernard Beckwith
Founder of the Agape International Spiritual Center

"Dr. Sha makes available secret techniques and insights that were available in the past only to a select few. He shares in simple terms the insights and tools that took him more than thirty years of hard work and discipline to attain. He gives you access to information that would otherwise be unattainable."
— Dr. John Gray
author of *Men Are from Mars, Women Are from Venus*

"Master Sha is the most important healer and teacher available in North America today. Master healers are rare. Here is one of the living masters of soul healing and its effects upon mind and body."
— Dr. C. Norman Shealy
author of *Life Beyond 100*

"Master Sha's unconditional love for humanity will open your heart and touch your soul. He is one of the most extraordinary and powerful human beings I have ever met."
— Barbara De Angelis
author of *Soul Shifts: Transformative Wisdom for Creating a Life of Authentic Awakening, Emotional Freedom and Practical Spirituality*

"Master Sha is divinely blessed and guided to heal the world and everything that is in it. From the smallest situation to the largest, he has the faithful gift of power to make things right. … His voice is like the voice of God singing."
— Roberta Flack
Grammy Award-winning musician

Published by Heaven's Library Publication Corp.
and Waterside Productions

Heaven's Library Publication Corp.
30 Wertheim Court, Unit 27D
Richmond Hill, ON L4B 1B9 Canada
www.heavenslibrary.com
heavenslibrary@drsha.com

Waterside Productions
2055 Oxford Ave.
Cardiff, CA 92007
www.waterside.com

ISBN: 978-1-957807-99-7 print-on-demand
ISBN: 978-1-958848-00-5 e-book

Design: Lynda Chaplin

Illustrations and cover: Henderson Ong

Animations: Hardeep Kharbanda, Yanan Wu

Contents

List of Figures   xiii

The Importance of Practice   xv

Foreword by William Gladstone with Gayle
    Gladstone   xvii

Introduction   xxiii

1. **Universal Law of Shen Qi Jing: A Soul Over
   Matter Information System**   1
       The Law of Shen Qi Jing Is a Law of Creation   4
       Five Steps of Creation   4
       The Law of Shen Qi Jing is a Law of Healing,
          Transformation, and Enlightenment   12

2. **Tao Science Explains the Universal Law of
   Shen Qi Jing**   17

3. **Why Do People Have Challenges in Health,
   Relationships, Finances, and Every Aspect
   of Life?**   25
       Positive Information, Energy, and Matter   27
       Negative Information, Energy, and Matter   29
       How to Transform Negative Information,
          Energy, and Matter   30

4. **Field**   33
       Positive Field   36
       Negative Field   36
       How to Transform a Negative Field to a
          Positive Field   36

5. **What Is Tao?**   **39**
    Tao Normal Creation   39
    Tao Reverse Creation   41
    The Ultimate Creator and Source   44
    What Is De?   49
    The Power and Significance of Tao and De   50

6. **Chinese Calligraphy**   **53**

7. **What Is Tao Calligraphy?**   **57**

8. **Tao Calligraphy Transformative Art Embodies
    the Ten Greatest Qualities to Transform and
    Enlighten Every Aspect of Life**   **59**
    Da Ai—Greatest Love: *Melts All Blockages and
        Transforms All Life*   63
    Da Kuan Shu—Greatest Forgiveness: *Brings
        Inner Joy and Inner Peace*   83
    Da Ci Bei—Greatest Compassion: *Boosts Energy,
        Stamina, Vitality, and Immunity, and
        Rejuvenates*   86
    Da Guang Ming—Greatest Light: *Heals and
        Transforms All Life*   89
    Da Qian Bei—Greatest Humility: *Prevents and
        Heals Ego in Order to Grow Persistently*   91
    Da He Xie—Greatest Harmony: *The Secret of
        Success*   94
    Da Chang Sheng—Greatest Flourishing:
        The Engine for Further Achievement   97
    Da Gan En—Greatest Gratitude: *The Key for
        Progress*   99

Da Fu Wu—Greatest Service: *The Purpose
        of Life*   101
Da Yuan Man—Greatest Enlightenment:
        The Ultimate Achievement for One's Life   106

9. **Tao Calligraphy Field Transformation**   **111**
    Tao Calligraphy *Da Ai* Field   112
    Tao Calligraphy *Da Ai* Field Transforms
        Health for the Physical Body   112
    Tao Calligraphy *Da Ai* Field Transforms
        Health for the Emotional Body   115
    Tao Calligraphy *Da Ai* Field Transforms
        Health for the Mental Body   117
    Tao Calligraphy *Da Ai* Field Transforms
        Health for the Spiritual Body   117
    Tao Calligraphy *Da Ai* Field Transforms
        Relationships   118
    Tao Calligraphy *Da Ai* Field Transforms
        Finances   121
    Zhong Mai Healing and Transformation   122
    Qi Channel   129

10. **Heal and Transform Depression and Anxiety
    with the Tao Calligraphy *Tao Zhuan You Yu
    Jiao Lü Field*   135**
    Xi Qing Hu Zhuo (Inhale Positive, Exhale
        Negative) Practice for Depression and
        Anxiety   138

11. **Heart-touching Stories of Tao Calligraphy Field
    Transformation of Depression and Anxiety   141**

12. Scientific Research on Tao Calligraphy Field
    Transformation of Depression
    by Peter Hudoba, M.D.   161

Conclusion   183

Upcoming Books in the Tao Calligraphy Series   185

List of Figures

1. Universal Law of Shen Qi Jing: Five Steps of Creation 8

2. Tao Normal Creation 40

3. Tao Reverse Creation 42

4. Tao Normal Creation and Tao Reverse Creation 43

5. Evolution and Styles of Six Basic Chinese Characters in Chinese Calligraphy 54

6. Six Basic Chinese Characters in Tao Oneness Calligraphy 55

7. Tao Calligraphy *Da Ai* (Greatest Love) 68

8. Five Elements 125

9. Seven Energy Chakras or Gears 126

10. San Jiao 127

11. Qi Channel and Wai Jiao 130

Tao Calligraphy *Tao Zhuan You Yu Jiao Lü* (Source Transforms Depression and Anxiety) ..... front and back covers

The Importance of Practice

THIS SECOND BOOK in my Tao Calligraphy book series includes soul-healing wisdom, knowledge, and practices for healing and transforming your health, relationships, finances, and more, with a focus in chapter ten on depression and anxiety.

The primary practice tool is Tao Calligraphy. Tao Calligraphy is Tao Source Oneness writing. It is art beyond art that can heal and transform your health, relationships, finances, spiritual journey, and every aspect of life.

Using two Tao Calligraphies that are included in this book, I will teach you how to practice in the Tao Calligraphy Field to heal and transform not only depression and anxiety, but any aspect of life. The practices are simple but profound. Practice is essential for healing and transformation of any aspect of life. Practice is vital for you to receive the greatest possible benefits that I wish you and every reader to receive.

Practice. Practice. Practice.
Heal. Heal. Heal.
Transform. Transform. Transform.

Access the practice videos

Use the URL below or scan the QR code with your smart-phone or other appropriate device to access the videos. A special app is not required.

https://tchtda.heavenslibrary.com

How to scan a QR code with your Android device
1. Launch the camera on your device.
2. Point it at the QR code.
3. Follow the instructions that appear on your screen.

How to scan a QR code with your iOS device
1. Launch the camera on your device.
2. Hold your device so that the QR code appears in the camera's viewfinder. Your device recognizes the QR code and shows a notification.
3. Tap the notification to open the link associated with the QR code.

Foreword

MY WIFE GAYLE and I have worked intimately with Dr. and Master Sha for a decade. I have personally agented several of his most important books, starting in 2013 with *Soul Healing Miracles*, which was an Amazon number one bestseller. To date, Master Sha has had eleven *New York Times* bestsellers, of which four reached number one.

In 2014, I wrote *Miracle Soul Healer: Exploring a Mystery*, a biography of Master Sha in which I investigated his healing practices and was able to confirm hundreds of "medical miracles." Dr. Peter Hudoba, a former neuroscientist, has globally led nineteen clinical studies of more than six hundred subjects applying Dr. and Master Sha's methods and practices. All research results in relevant studies showed significant improvements in wellbeing.

I have a graduate degree in medical anthropology from Harvard University. One of my early scientific studies was published in the magazine *Yale Scientific* when I was a Yale undergraduate. I can confirm that the healings attributed to Master Sha and his trained healers far exceed any statistical correlation that could be attributed to the placebo effect. Although the precise mechanism for Master Sha's amazing results may defy current scientific explanation, new findings in quantum physics and other fields which are creating the new paradigm of "post materialist science" may offer insights into the understanding of what until now has remained a scientific mystery and anomaly.

Master Sha maintains that the mystery of his healing abilities can be understood by an analysis of Tao (phonetically, *Dao*). This book explains in depth the nature of Tao. Tao is Source. Every element of life is contained within the Tao. You will learn how this works in this wonderful book.

When Master Sha first contacted me to be his literary agent, he did so because of my success with well-known spiritual authors and visionaries such as Eckhart Tolle, Neale Donald Walsch, Barbara Marx Hubbard, Barbara DeAngelis, Deepak Chopra, and many others. When we first spoke, Master Sha was most impressed by the success my company, Waterside Productions, Inc., had had in creating the For Dummies book series now published by John Wiley. As his publisher for ten years, my goal is for Master Sha to create a book series as popular and simple as the For Dummies series or the Chicken Soup for the Soul book series created by my friends Jack Canfield and Mark Victor Hansen. Both of these series have sold in excess of five hundred million copies. Gayle and I both believe Master Sha's Tao Calligraphy book series can reach this level of popularity. Although this and future titles in the Tao Calligraphy series require a greater commitment from readers to fully understand the principles presented than either of those two phenomenal book series mentioned, they are on another level even more accessible and should be even more popular.

Gayle and I believe this for several reasons. First, and most amazing, readers can benefit from these books without even reading them. Each book will include one or more Tao Calligraphies, unique works of art that carry a Source quantum vibrational field designed to transform specific ailments or improve specific life situations. This second volume you are reading addresses issues of anxiety and depression. If you have issues of anxiety or depression, just hold the Tao Calligraphy image on the front or back cover over your heart! You could receive relief and, for some, even recovery. You may or may not believe this is possible but try it. Not everyone will have an immediate positive reaction but many will. Master Sha never promises any result of any kind with any of his healing techniques and he always encourages everyone to consult healthcare professionals and continue with traditional medical regimens. This book is not a substitute for medical treatment. It is however a supplemental approach that has helped hundreds of thousands with no negative side effects. Five years ago, Gayle's daughter was diagnosed with fourth stage breast cancer and was gifted a healing calligraphy by Master Sha. The medical team was astonished when she showed no signs of cancer just a few months later. Her primary treatment modality was tracing the calligraphy and listening to Master Sha's Tao Song audio recording. Both Gayle and I were in disbelief but extremely grateful. Her daughter remains cancer-free to this day.

As Master Sha quotes from ancient Chinese wisdom: "If you want to know if a pear is sweet, taste it." Gayle and I strongly encourage you to taste this book. If you do have a positive experience, either immediately or over time as you continue to do the practices and study the wisdom, we would be delighted to hear from you. Please email your comments to TaoCalligraphyField@DrSha.com.

For those of you who want to truly understand the essence of Tao healing and why Tao Calligraphy has become such an effective healing modality, this is the best possible book for you to read. Gayle suggests that the first time you read this book, you skip the Chinese characters and focus on the practical exercises and summary conclusions provided in each chapter. For those wanting to go deeper, read the book a second time and focus on the Chinese characters and how they have been translated to English. Those who do this second reading will be greatly rewarded. Chinese calligraphy is a tradition that dates back thousands of years. The Chinese systems of Tao and energy healing date back to even earlier millennia. The wisdom Dr. and Master Sha has gathered from his studies and practices over the last six decades is unique. No other teacher or visionary on planet Earth at this time has developed such a clear explanation of why you can heal yourself once you learn to access Tao, the ultimate source of all creation. No other teacher gives you such simple and practical yet powerful tools and techniques for self-healing and self-transformation.

Master Sha's mission is to teach each of us that we can heal ourselves, we can heal others, and together we can heal our precious planet Earth. Use this book and share it with your circle of family and friends. In doing so, you will be contributing to your own wellbeing and that of our global community.

With best wishes for you to experience joy and accomplishment in every aspect of life.

William Gladstone with Gayle Gladstone, publishers of Waterside books, audios, non-fungible tokens, and online courses

Introduction

THE PURPOSE OF LIFE is to serve. I have committed my life to this purpose. To serve is to make others happier and healthier. To serve is to empower and enlighten others.

Millions of people have health challenges. A human being has four bodies: physical, emotional, mental, and spiritual. Human beings have countless health challenges in all four bodies.

Millions of people have relationship challenges with partners, children, parents, friends, colleagues, communities, companies, cities, countries, belief systems, and more.

Millions of people have financial or business challenges that can involve unemployment, debt, childcare, commuting, employee relationships, company structure and plans, financial controls, marketing, competitors, customers, suppliers, efficiency, effectiveness, and more.

Throughout the world, millions of people have major challenges in every aspect of life—with the environment, natural disasters, illness, COVID-19, the economy, politics, war, fear, pain, depression, anxiety, and more.

Millions of people are studying and searching for transformation toward solutions to all kinds of current challenges and conditions.

Why are Mother Earth and humanity suffering now?

Is there any way to transform all of these challenges?

If so, what is the way and how can we use it to transform the challenges?

This book will answer these questions and more. Most important, this book will offer practical techniques to transform the challenges.

In ancient Chinese wisdom, there is a renowned sacred teaching: da Dao zhi jian 大道至简. This means *the greatest Tao is extremely simple.*

Tao is the Ultimate Creator and Source. Tao carries Source love and light. Tao carries Source frequency and vibration. Tao carries Source most-positive information, energy, and matter, which could transform any and all negative information, energy, and matter in every aspect of life. Tao has infinite abilities. Tao carries the highest power of *soul over matter*, which is soulfulness. Soul over matter means *soul can make things happen.* Soul can transform every aspect of life, including health, relationships, finances, and the spiritual journey.

Another important ancient Chinese phrase is shu yi zai Dao 书以载道. This means *calligraphy is used to carry Tao.*

This book, *Tao Calligraphy to Heal and Transform Depression and Anxiety*, will apply shu yi zai Dao through Tao Calligraphy Transformative Art. This unique form of Chinese calligraphy carries a Tao Source field, which is Tao Source information, energy, matter, frequency, and vibration, to serve humanity and Mother Earth.

I will also introduce the universal law that is the law of creation, healing, transformation, and enlightenment for every aspect of life. This law of creation is the "soul over matter" information system governing everyone and everything.

I will share the ten greatest qualities carried within Tao Calligraphy Transformative Art to transform and enlighten all life.

I wish this book will serve you to transform challenges in your life.

I wish this book will serve you to transform challenges in your family.

I wish this book will serve humanity to transform challenges in society.

I wish this book will serve countless souls to transform challenges for cities, countries, and Mother Earth.

I love my heart and soul
I love all humanity
Join hearts and souls together
Love, peace, and harmony
Love, peace, and harmony

Universal Law of Shen Qi Jing: A Soul Over Matter Information System

THERE IS GREAT ancient wisdom within three words: jing qi shen 精氣神. The *Yellow Emperor's Inner Canon* 黃帝內經, the earliest authoritative book of traditional Chinese medicine, explains jing is *matter*; qi is *energy*; and shen is *soul* or *spirit*, which is expressed through energy and matter.

Everyone and everything are made of shen qi jing.[1] A human being, an animal, a house, an ocean, a mountain, Mother Earth, and countless planets, stars, galaxies, and universes are all made of shen qi jing.

Generally speaking, we can see matter and feel energy, but we cannot see the soul. For example, if we are on the shore by an ocean, we could feel the ocean's energy. If we are on a mountain, we could feel the mountain's energy. Under

---

[1] I reverse the traditional order of jing qi shen to shen qi jing because, as I will explain, the soul is the boss.

1

the sun, we can feel the sun's energy. However, most people cannot see the soul of an ocean, a mountain, or the sun because the soul is a light being. A soul's light is beyond the spectrum of visible light. Even a highly-developed spiritual being with open spiritual channels may not be able to see souls.

Dr. Rulin Xiu, a quantum physicist and string theorist, co-founded Tao Science[2] with me. Tao Science shares that shen qi jing is a universal law, just as the Law of Yin Yang and the Law of Five Elements are universal laws, which means that they apply to and describe everyone and everything in countless planets, stars, galaxies, and universes.

The Universal Law of Shen Qi Jing is the first foundational law of Tao Science. This law states that:

**Everyone and everything are
made of shen, qi, and jing.**

Shen includes soul, heart, and mind. This heart is more than the physical heart. This heart is the core of life.

Qi is energy.

Jing is matter.

Because energy and matter make up the body, we can re-state the Law of Shen Qi Jing as follows:

---

[2] See Zhi Gang Sha and Rulin Xiu, *Tao Science: The Science, Wisdom, and Practice of Creation and Grand Unification* (Cardiff, California/Richmond Hill, Ontario: Waterside Press/ Heaven's Library Publication Corp., 2017).

Everyone and everything have a
soul, heart, mind, and body.

Einstein's renowned equation, $E = mc^2$, states the relationship between the energy (E) and mass (m) of a body of matter. Tao Science states the relationship among soul, energy, and matter via the equation:

$$S + E + M = 1$$

In this equation, "S" represents shen, which includes soul, heart, and mind.

"E" represents qi or energy.

"M" represents jing or matter.

"1" represents the Tao Source Oneness Field.

Dr. Rulin Xiu and I feel that the Tao Source Oneness Field is the grand unified field that physicists have been seeking for decades in order to develop a grand unification theory that encompasses all known fields and forces in space and time. I will explain the Tao Source Oneness Field further in subsequent chapters.

The equation $S + E + M = 1$ expresses that one's soul, heart, and mind, plus energy and matter, are in a Oneness field. If this Oneness field is broken, then any challenges in all life could appear, whether in health, relationships, finances, the spiritual journey, or any other aspect.

To heal, transform, and enlighten every aspect of life is to align one's soul, heart, mind, energy, and matter as one. This is a universal law and the ultimate truth for all life.

The Law of Shen Qi Jing Is a Law of Creation

In this book some major wisdom, concepts, and practices are emphasized and repeated. The purpose is to help you realize their importance and to imprint them in your heart and soul.

Shen includes soul, heart, and mind. Soul is information or message. The Law of Shen Qi Jing describes a soul over matter information system. This soul over matter information system describes the process of creation, which has five steps.

Five Steps of Creation

The five steps of creation are:

Step 1. Soul is information, which is a creator.

The concept and study of information are key in quantum physics and Tao Science. In simple terms, if we think of everyone and everything as a computer network, information is like the data input that determines the output, including the characteristics, behavior, and nature of a system.

In spiritual terms, information or message is soul. For everyone and everything, the soul is the warehouse of information. For example, a person's soul is the warehouse of all the information or messages the person has accumulated in current and past lifetimes.

The information stored by the soul is a creator. "Soul over matter" means *the soul can make things happen*. In fact, the soul can transform every aspect of life.

Step 2. Soul leads the heart.

Everyone and everything have a heart. This heart is more than the physical heart. This heart is the physical heart, the emotional heart, the spiritual heart, and more. A human has a heart. An animal has a heart. Does an ocean have a heart? Does a mountain have a heart? Does Mother Earth have a heart? Yes! They all have a heart. This heart is the receiver of the information stored by the soul. This heart is the core of life.

Step 3. Heart leads the mind.

Mind is consciousness. It includes superficial consciousness, deep consciousness, subconsciousness, logical consciousness, imaginal consciousness, inspirational consciousness, huge consciousness, and more.

Consciousness is a big subject to study. Millions of people apply mind over matter, which is mindfulness. This means the mind can make things happen. Millions of people meditate. Millions of people use positive thinking.

Millions of people use positive chanting, such as affirmations. These practices all belong to mind over matter or mindfulness.

Mind is the processor. Think about a factory. In the chain of production, raw or unassembled material is input. At the end of the chain, the output is the finished product. Similarly, the input that the mind receives is information or messages from the soul, via the heart. The mind processes this information, consciously or subconsciously, and then makes a decision—consciously or subconsciously—as its "finished product."

Mind over matter and mindfulness are great. But in my personal opinion, they are not enough. People may not be aware that mindfulness is directed by the heart. We could move to heart over matter or heartfulness. Heartfulness would be a level beyond mindfulness. In ancient wisdom, the heart houses the mind and soul. The ultimate level is soulfulness, which is soul over matter. Soul over matter is the core teaching in all of my books and I apply it in all of the practices I share.

Step 4. Mind leads energy.

Energy is the mover. Energy drives matter. In the human body, energy drives blood. One fundamental tenet of traditional Chinese medicine since its inception five thousand years ago is:

> **If qi (energy) flows, blood flows.**
> **If qi is blocked, blood is stagnant.**

In the understanding of traditional Chinese medicine, all cysts, tumors, and cancers are due to qi blockages. There is an ancient statement:

qi ju ze cheng xing, qi san ze cheng feng
氣聚則成形, 氣散則成风

Qi means *energy*. Ju means *to accumulate*. Ze is a conjunction indicating causation. Cheng means *to become*. Xing means *shape*. Qi ju ze cheng xing means *qi accumulates to form a shape*. This is how a cyst, a tumor, and cancer are formed.

San means *to disperse*. Feng means *wind*. Qi san ze cheng feng means *qi disperses like the wind flowing away*.

Millions of people meditate. Meditation is at the mind level. Mind directs energy. For example, if in your meditation you focus on your kidneys, your energy will move toward the kidneys. Mind leads energy.

Step 5. Energy leads matter.

Blood is matter. If energy flows, blood flows. If a person sprains an ankle, the skin, muscles, tendons, and even the bones around the ankle could be injured. The blood is stagnant. Blood stagnation causes pain and makes movement difficult.

Matter manifests the information in our physical reality. It can transform the information.

Figure 1 summarizes the five steps of creation in the Universal Law of Shen Qi Jing.

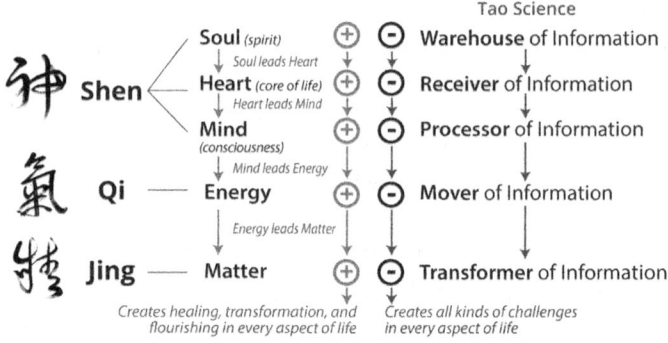

Figure 1. Universal Law of Shen Qi Jing: Five Steps of Creation

The five steps of creation from the Law of Shen Qi Jing are vital for every aspect of life. More than sixteen years ago, on Saturday, September 10, 2005, I was with three of my trained soul-healing teachers and healers at Muir Woods National Monument just north of San Francisco. There, I asked the Divine directly, "Dear Divine, could you give me a song for healing?"

Instantly I could see with my spiritual eye a beam of rainbow light flowing down from Heaven into and through my whole body, from head to toe. Then, I opened my mouth. The following sounds flowed out:

Lu La Lu La Li
Lu La Lu La La Li
Lu La Lu La Li Lu La
Lu La Li Lu La
Lu La Li Lu La

I knew right away this was the Divine's soul voice and language. The Divine told me that he is giving me one of his songs and with that I received the melody.

I asked the Divine to give me the meaning of this soul language and song. I received a translation in Chinese, my native language, first:

wo ai wo xin he ling 我愛我心和靈
wo ai quan ren lei 我愛全人类
wan ling rong he mu shi sheng 萬靈融合睦世生
xiang ai ping an he xie 相愛平安和谐
xiang ai ping an he xie 相愛平安和谐

Let me explain line by line.

wo ai wo xin he ling
Wo means *I* or *my*. Ai means *to love*. Xin means *heart*. He means *and*. Ling means *soul*. Wo ai wo xin he ling means *I love my heart and soul*.

wo ai quan ren lei
Quan means *entire*. Ren lei means *humanity*. Wo ai quan ren lei means *I love all humanity*.

wan ling rong he mu shi sheng
Wan ling means *all souls*. Rong he means *meld as one*. Mu shi means *harmonious world*. Sheng means *to create* or *to give birth to*. Wan ling rong he mu shi sheng means *all souls meld as one to create a harmonious world*.

xiang ai ping an he xie
Xiang ai means *love*. Ping an means *peace*. He xie means *harmony*. Xiang ai ping an he xie means *love, peace, harmony*.

Then, the Divine gave me the English translation to be sung to his melody:

I love my heart and soul
I love all humanity
Join hearts and souls together
Love, peace, and harmony
Love, peace, and harmony

The Divine Soul Song "Love, Peace, and Harmony" has created hundreds of thousands of heart-touching and amazing results for healing and transformation, including for health, relationships, finances, the spiritual journey, and every aspect of life.

This Divine Soul Song explains and embodies the five steps of creation from the Law of Shen Qi Jing very well.

Step 1. Soul is information or message, which is a creator.

The process of soul over matter is: soul leads heart; heart leads mind; mind leads energy; energy leads blood, which is matter.

Every line, every word of this Divine Soul Song is information. The entire Divine Soul Song is a powerful accumulation of the positive information of each line.

I love my heart and soul
I love all humanity
Join hearts and souls together
Love, peace, and harmony
Love, peace, and harmony

This information is a creator.

Step 2. Soul leads the heart.

Soul passes the information or message to the heart. The heart is the receiver of the information. When we sing or even listen to this Divine Soul Song, our heart receives its information or message. The more open and clear our heart is, the more fully and deeply our heart will receive the information or message of "Love, Peace, and Harmony."

Step 3. Heart leads the mind.

Our heart passes the information or message to our mind. The mind receives the information or message and processes it.

Step 4. Mind leads energy.

The mind then passes the information to our energy. The energy moves.

Step 5. Energy leads matter.

Energy moves matter. Matter transforms. Blood is matter. Energy drives blood to flow more fluidly. Then, we are healing and transforming.

The Law of Shen Qi Jing is a law of creation that can explain any creation process. I am delighted to release this new wisdom that the Universal Law of Shen Qi Jing is a law of creation for humanity and Mother Earth.

The Law of Shen Qi Jing is a Law of Healing, Transformation, and Enlightenment

The Universal Law of Shen Qi Jing is also a law of healing, transformation, and enlightenment.

I released the Say Hello soul-healing technique sixteen years ago in my book, *Soul Mind Body Medicine*.[3] Twelve years ago, I traveled to India to teach soul healing. In one of my workshops, a medical doctor came to the stage and shared two soul-healing stories from his patients.

The first story was about a woman who had suffered from serious psoriasis for seven years. Her whole body was inflamed and shedding dry, flaky skin. The doctor, a family physician, guided this woman to do my Say Hello soul-healing practice. He taught her to say:

> *Dear soul, mind, and body of my skin,*
> *I love you.*
> *You have the power to heal yourself.*
> *Do a good job!*
> *Thank you.*

---

[3] Zhi Gang Sha, *Soul Mind Body Medicine: A Complete Soul Healing System for Optimum Health and Vitality* (Novato, California: New World Library, 2006).

This woman repeated this Say Hello soul-healing formula, which I named Soul Power—the power of soul over matter—from morning to night. Within two days, the inflammation was completely gone. Within seven days, the skin on her whole body was cleared and returned to a normal appearance. This doctor was so impressed that he immediately purchased all of my available books at that time, saying he was eager to read all of them.

The Say Hello soul-healing technique is soul over matter.

The doctor's second story was about a woman who suffered from a large mass (about five inches across) on her uterus. The physician also told her to repeat the Say Hello soul-healing technique and formula:

Dear soul, mind, and body of my uterus,
I love you.
You have the power to heal yourself.
Do a good job!
Thank you.

This woman repeated the Say Hello formula for a total of more than two hours a day.

I have taught for decades that people who suffer from chronic pain or life-threatening conditions need to do soul-healing practices for at least two hours per day. There is no time limit. The longer one practices, the better the results one could receive. Practice can be done in shorter segments. I recommend at least twenty minutes per practice session. For very serious and life-threatening conditions, total daily practice time (in however many individual practice sessions) should be at least two hours.

The woman with the uterine tumor practiced for two hours or more a day. After three weeks, her tumor disappeared. The physician said in my workshop that he could hardly believe what had happened for the two women just by repeating the Say Hello soul-healing formula.

These two stories demonstrate that the Universal Law of Shen Qi Jing is also a law of healing and transformation. How? It is easy to understand. The five steps of creation in the Universal Law of Shen Qi Jing can create healing and transformation.

Step 1. Soul is information or message, which is a creator.

The Say Hello soul-healing technique and formula is the information that is a creator.

Step 2. Soul leads the heart.

Every skin cell has a soul. Every skin cell has a heart. Every uterine tumor cell has a soul. Every uterine tumor cell has a heart. The hearts of the skin, skin cells, uterus, uterus cells, uterine tumor, and uterine tumor cells receive the healing information of the Say Hello soul-healing technique. The hearts of the cells pass the information to the minds or consciousness of the skin and uterus cells.

Step 3. Heart leads the mind.

Every cell of the skin, uterus, and uterine tumor has a mind. The minds of the cells receive the healing information from the hearts of the cells. The minds process and then pass the information to the energy.

Step 4. Mind leads energy.

The energy receives the healing information from the minds and moves. This energy movement drives the matter.

Step 5. Energy leads matter.

Blood is matter. The energy drives the blood. Blood flows better. All the biochemical behavior in the body could transform at the cellular level. The matter of the skin and the uterine tumor could transform at the cellular level. Thus, the two women recovered completely in a short time.

Humanity suffers from many sicknesses. Soul-healing techniques, which are soul over matter, apply the Universal Law of Shen Qi Jing as a law of creation, as a law of healing and transformation, and as a law of enlightenment (because it can heal and transform one's spiritual journey). We have received literally thousands of heart-touching and moving results from those applying the Say Hello soul-healing and transformation technique for healing of the physical body, emotional body, mental body, and spiritual body, as well as for transforming relationships and finances.

Peter Hudoba, a medical doctor and neuroscientist, has led numerous clinical research studies on a total of more than six hundred subjects on the effects of soul-healing techniques, including Tao Source soul healing, for various conditions. Chapter twelve shares some of this medical research on subjects with depression or anxiety.

Tao Science Explains the Universal Law of Shen Qi Jing

D R. RULIN XIU and I co-created Tao Science in 2016.

Dr. Xiu is a quantum physicist and string theorist, having received her Ph.D. in 1994 from the University of California at Berkeley. She is also an entrepreneur, herbalist, singer, author, and a Master Teacher and Healer trained by my Tao Academy and me. Tao Science is the culmination of her three decades of work on a grand unification theory.

Tao is the Source of everyone and everything. Tao Science is the science of the Source, creation, healing, transformation, and enlightenment. Tao Science is a new groundbreaking science that helps unify science and spirituality at the most fundamental level. Tao Science is the science of grand unification.

According to ancient Chinese wisdom, which is part of the Universal Law of Shen Qi Jing, everyone and everything are made of three things: shen (soul, heart, and mind), qi (energy), and jing (matter).

Scientific research reveals that these three basic constituents of everyone and everything—shen, qi, and jing—generally correspond to three scientific concepts: information, energy, and matter.

Matter is what we see, hear, feel, observe, and experience. It is everything in our physical reality.

Energy is what changes and moves matter.

Information is what determines the form and shape of matter and energy. It is that which informs. To inform is to answer a question. Questions can be posed so that the answer is either "yes" or "no." Therefore, information can be represented as a sequence of yesses and nos. A computer does exactly this by specifying information using a series of 0s and 1s. Living in the information age, we know the importance of this. For example, we know that the information about our bank account determines how much money we can withdraw from it.

Modern physics reveals that everyone and everything is a vibrational field. A vibration, also called a wave, is a periodic oscillation extending over space and time. A vibration is described by its frequency, wavelength, amplitude, and velocity. Frequency describes how fast the vibration oscillates. Wavelength is the distance between two adjacent peaks of the vibration. Amplitude tells us the height of the oscillation. Velocity shows the speed at which the vibration travels. Our vibrational field contains many different vibrations. It carries information, energy, and matter.

Although everything we observe and experience is matter, it takes energy to move and change matter, and it is information that determines energy and matter. Information determines and creates what we observe and experience. Information in our vibrational field determines every aspect of our life.

Information consists of three aspects: content of information, receiver and emitter of information, and processor of information.

We find that the content of information in our vibrational field is spirit or soul. Because the content of information determines every aspect of life, spirit or soul is the essence of our life. It plays a critical role in shaping our life. When our physical body ceases to function, the content of information in our vibrational field still exists. That is why our spirit or soul continues its journey even when our physical life ends.

Physical life is limited. Spirit or soul can be eternal. Physical life is determined and directed by the spirit or soul. The highest purpose of our physical life is to serve our soul's purpose. Our soul has its purpose. When we know our soul's purpose, our physical life can be smoother and have greater meaning and impact.

We have a physical heart and a spiritual heart. The spiritual heart is the heart mentioned in spiritual writings. We have discovered that the spiritual heart is the receiver and emitter of information. The antenna of a radio is a receiver of information. It can receive the vibrations and information of a radio program transmitted from a radio station, making it possible for us to hear the broadcast. Similarly, our spiritual heart, the receiver and emitter of information, makes it possible to manifest the information from our soul into our reality. Without applying our spiritual heart, we would not be able to receive all of the positive information from our soul to empower us to manifest a life we want.

Mind is the processor of information. Similar to a computer, our mind can process information received from our spiritual heart. The output of this process is a decision, which could be conscious or subconscious. With this decision, the mind tells us what action to take. In this way, mind directs energy and changes the matter, our physical reality.

In our research, we have discovered that there are two kinds of information: positive and negative.

Positive information describes the connection, order, and harmony existing within someone or something and with others. Positive information gives a soul the power to create simply by giving a message. Positive information brings health, longevity, peace, efficiency, good relationships, abundant finances, and success in every aspect of life. A happy, healthy, and successful life is built on a solid foundation of positive information. Therefore, the purpose of life is to enhance our positive information.

Negative information is the disconnection, disorder, and disharmony within someone or something and with others. Negative information generates sickness, unbalanced emotions, inefficiency, difficulties in relationships, blockages in finances, and lack of success in any aspect of life. Negative information is the root cause of all diseases, misfortune, and challenges in life.

In one sentence:

**Information is the root cause of
success and failure in any aspect of life.**

Positive information is the root cause of success. Negative information is the root cause of failure. Therefore, to heal, transform, empower, and uplift our life at the deepest root level is to turn negative information in our vibrational field into positive information.

Everyone and everything are an information system. Our soul, heart, and mind are three important aspects of our information system, which molds every aspect of our life. From the point of view of information, energy is the actioner of information. Matter is the manifester and transformer of information. Our physical life is the manifestation of our soul's information. What we experience in our life and how we experience it tells our soul the consequences of the information it carries through our heart, mind, and body. The purpose of our physical life is to help our soul learn, transform, and be uplifted to a higher level of positive information.

When we give a specific message or information, the specific information starts to attract and direct energy and matter and leads to the phenomena we observe and experience. This is how we create our own reality and our own life.

The Law of Shen Qi Jing is a law of cause and effect. Information, including soul, heart, and mind, is the cause. Our physical reality is the effect of the information. This tells us how we ourselves create every aspect of our life from the information we give and receive through thinking, feeling, speaking, hearing, seeing, writing, and other actions.

If we want to create a life we truly want, we should be disciplined to think, feel, speak, hear, see, write, and convey the proper information, which is positive information or positive messages, about what we want in life. If we think, feel, speak, hear, see, write, and convey information about what we don't want, which is negative information, we will experience what we don't want. This is why we need to stop thinking, feeling, speaking, hearing, seeing, writing, and doing things that convey information about what we don't want.

Five sacred phrases tell us to avoid receiving and creating negative information:

mu bu wang shi 目不妄视
er bu wang ting 耳不妄听
kou bu wang yan 口不妄言
nao bu wang xiang 脑不妄想
xin wu gua ai 心无挂碍

These mean:

Eyes do not see negative things.
Ears do not hear negative words or sounds.
Mouth does not speak negative words.
Mind does not think negative thoughts.
Heart is not concerned or disturbed.

Buddha taught "xin wu gua ai" 心无挂碍. Xin means *heart*. Wu means *not*. Gua ai means *to be concerned* or *to worry*. All concerns and worries convey negative information, which creates the reality of what we worry about. When our heart does not have any concerns, worries, fears, grief, anger, sense of lack, depression, or any negativity, we can create and enjoy a life we want. Xin wu gua ai is important wisdom and a practice to create a life we want.

ဢ ဢ ღ

The source of everyone and everything is emptiness. In physics, emptiness is called a vacuum. Emptiness has no shape or form. It has no space or time. Quantum physics tells us that within a vacuum or emptiness there are infinite possibilities and infinite information, energy, and matter. Everyone and everything come from the Source.

Source is connected with everyone and everything. This is why Source has pure positive information, energy, and matter.

The beauty and power of this book come from connecting with a Tao Source field to receive Source frequency and vibration; Source most-positive information, energy, and matter; and Source highest power of soul over matter to heal and transform our negative fields of negative information, energy, and matter.

Why Do People Have Challenges in Health, Relationships, Finances, and Every Aspect of Life?

MILLIONS OF PEOPLE suffer from sickness in the physical body, including all kinds of pain, inflammation, cysts, tumors, cancer, COVID-19, and many other sicknesses.

Millions of people suffer from sickness in the emotional body, including anger, depression, anxiety, worry, grief, fear, guilt, shame, loneliness, and more.

Millions of people suffer from sickness in the mental body, including poor concentration, diminishing memory, negative thinking, judgment, ego, and many mental disorders, such as schizophrenia, OCD, PTSD, and more.

Millions of people suffer from sickness in the spiritual body, because the soul can carry negative information. In fact, as we have seen in the Universal Law of Shen Qi Jing, negative information is the root cause of all kinds of sickness in the physical, emotional, mental, and spiritual bodies.

Millions of people have relationship challenges, including with partners, parents, children, siblings, other relatives, friends, bosses, employees, colleagues, organizations, and more.

Organizations, belief systems, cities, countries, and more could also have relationship challenges with each other.

Millions of people have environmental challenges, including polluted air, water, or land, inadequate shelter, unhealthy food, lack of healthcare, and more.

Millions of people have financial challenges.

Why do we have so many challenges in every aspect of life?

What is the key to understanding all of these challenges?

Is there a solution for these challenges?

If so, what is the solution?

I wrote this book to answer these four questions. Above all, I wrote this book to serve you, humanity, and Mother Earth.

In one sentence:

Humanity has all kinds of challenges in health, relationships, finances, the spiritual journey, and every aspect of life because of negative information, energy, and matter (negative shen qi jing).

What is the key to understanding all of these challenges? In one sentence, the key is that the heart and the soul are affected and influenced by negative information, energy, and matter.

Is there a solution for these challenges? In one sentence, the solution to all challenges in health, relationships, finances, the spiritual journey, and every aspect of life is to apply positive information, energy, and matter (positive shen qi jing) to transform negative information, energy, and matter.

Positive Information, Energy, and Matter

Tao Science states that information, energy, and matter can be positive or negative. This revolutionary insight helps us deeply understand sickness, healing, and transformation. What are positive information, energy, and matter? Positive information, energy, and matter are any information, energy, or matter that promotes order, connection, and harmony. Positive information, energy, and matter can heal and transform sickness, prevent sickness, rejuvenate, prolong life, harmonize relationships, boost finances and business, and enlighten one's spiritual journey.

There are ten qualities that carry the most-positive information, energy, and matter: greatest love, greatest forgiveness, greatest compassion, greatest light, greatest humility, greatest harmony, greatest flourishing, greatest gratitude, greatest service, and greatest enlightenment. I will explain these ten greatest qualities in more detail in chapter eight.

Because these ten greatest qualities are the most-positive information, energy, and matter, they can transform every aspect of life. They are the highest wisdom. At the same time, they are the highest practice. They carry the highest power.

In ancient wisdom, shu yi zai Dao 书以载道, which means *calligraphy is used to carry Tao*. In this book, I share two Tao Calligraphies I have written to carry some of the ten greatest qualities to serve you, as well as to serve families, humanity, organizations, cities, countries, and Mother Earth.

Tao Calligraphy is Tao Source Oneness writing. It is art. It is art beyond art that can heal and transform health, relationships, finances, the spiritual journey, and every aspect of life. I will teach you how to practice in the Tao Calligraphy Field to transform every aspect of life. The practices are simple but profound. Practice is vital for you to receive the greatest possible benefits that I wish you and every reader to receive.

In one sentence:

All good health, harmonious relationships, flourishing finances and business, and enlightened spiritual journeys are due to positive information, energy, and matter.

Negative Information, Energy, and Matter

What are negative information, energy, and matter? Negative information, energy, and matter are any information, energy, or matter that promotes disorder, disconnection, and disharmony. Negative information, energy, and matter cause sickness, relationship challenges, and financial challenges. Negative information, energy, and matter block one's spiritual journey. Negative information, energy, and matter create blockages in every aspect of life.

A human being has physical, emotional, mental, and spiritual bodies.

In the physical body, any lack of energy, vitality, or stamina; any pain, inflammation, cysts, tumors, or cancer; and all other sicknesses are negative information, energy, and matter.

In the emotional body, anger, depression, anxiety, guilt, shame, worry, grief, fear, and more are negative information, energy, and matter.

In the mental body, confusion, mental disorders, poor concentration, poor memory, ego, and more are negative information, energy, and matter.

In the spiritual body, not understanding or realizing the importance of the soul journey, which is the spiritual journey, getting lost on one's spiritual journey, creating mistakes of hurting and harming others and the environment, and more are negative information, energy, and matter.

For relationships, any disharmony in any kind of relationship is negative information, energy, and matter.

For finances, all blockages in any aspect of finances are negative information, energy, and matter.

For a business, any challenge in any part of the business is negative information, energy, and matter.

In one sentence:

All challenges, blockages, and failures in health, relationships, finances, and the spiritual journey are due to negative information, energy, and matter.

How to Transform Negative Information, Energy, and Matter

To transform all challenges in health, relationships, finances, the spiritual journey, and every aspect of life is to transform negative information, energy, and matter to positive information, energy, and matter.

I am delighted to offer a Tao Source practical tool to help you, families, society, organizations, humanity, and Mother Earth. This practical tool is named Tao Calligraphy.

Tao Calligraphy creates and carries an Ultimate Source most-positive field, which could transform negative fields in all life, including health, relationships, finances, and the spiritual journey. Health includes four bodies: physical, emotional, mental, and spiritual. I continue to explain the Tao Calligraphy Field in the next chapter.

Field

THE ENGLISH PHYSICIST and chemist Michael Faraday coined the term "field" in 1849.

Scientists and others have identified and studied many kinds of fields, such as:

- electric
- magnetic
- electromagnetic
- gravitational
- temperature
- velocity flow
- quantum
- and more

In 1920, Albert Einstein realized that the concept of field, specifically a gravitational field, is a more accurate way to describe gravity than as a force. Finally, Einstein emphasized that there is only one real thing in the universe, which is a field.

Quantum physics discovered that everyone and everything is fundamentally a vibrational field made of various vibrations. A vibration, also called a wave, is a periodic oscillation extending over space and time. Quantum physics further reveals that our vibrational field determines our qualities and life experiences. To be a person of good quality and to experience a good life, we need to have a good vibrational field.

A good vibrational field is one carrying positive information, energy, and matter. Positive information, energy, and matter bring connection, order, and harmony. They are the cause of good health, harmonious relationships, and success in finances and careers. A bad vibrational field is one carrying negative information, energy, and matter. Negative information, energy, and matter bring disconnection, disorder, and disharmony. They are the cause of sickness, difficulties, challenges, and disasters.

To transform negative information, energy, and matter in one's vibrational field to positive information, energy, and matter is to heal sickness, overcome adversity, and turn lack into abundance at the root level.

Tao is the Ultimate Creator and Source. The vibrational field of Tao Source contains unlimited positive information, energy, and matter. Tao Source can create anything. It can provide for, support, and nourish everyone and everything. To connect with the Source vibrational field is the highest and most powerful way to heal, transform, and empower ourselves.

This book shares with humanity that the Tao Calligraphy Field is a Tao Source field, that the Tao Calligraphy Field exists, and that the Tao Calligraphy Field is available to serve you now.

In chapter one, I explained the Universal Law of Shen Qi Jing, which is a law of creation, a law of healing, a law of transformation, and a law of enlightenment. Shen qi jing form a field.

A human being is made of shen qi jing, which is soul, heart, mind, energy, and matter. A human being's shen qi jing form a human being's field.

An ocean is made of shen qi jing, which form an ocean's field.

Mother Earth is made of shen qi jing, which form Mother Earth's field.

A solar system has its own shen qi jing, which form a solar system's field.

In summary:

Everyone and everything in countless planets, stars, galaxies, and universes are made of their own shen qi jing. Their own shen qi jing form their own field.

Countless planets, stars, galaxies, and universes have both positive and negative shen qi jing, which are their positive and negative fields.

Positive Field

Any field that brings good health, harmonious relationships, flourishing finances, progress on the spiritual journey, or love, peace, and harmony to humanity, Mother Earth, and countless planets, stars, galaxies, and universes is a positive field.

Negative Field

Any field that causes unhealthy conditions for humanity, unharmonious relationships, blockages in finances, challenges on the spiritual journey, or reduces love, peace, and harmony for humanity, Mother Earth, and countless planets, stars, galaxies, and universes is a negative field.

The Universal Law of Shen Qi Jing tells us that positive shen qi jing could transform negative shen qi jing. In other words, a positive field could transform a negative field in health, relationships, finances, the spiritual journey, and every aspect of life.

How to Transform a Negative Field to a Positive Field

There are many ways to transform a negative field to a positive field.

In medicine, doctors, nurses, hospitals, and more help people to heal. They are transforming negative fields to positive fields.

People eat food and drink water. People realize that eating proper food and drinking healthy water are vital for life. When we do this, we are strengthening our positive field. We should avoid unhealthy foods and polluted water because they carry negative fields.

All kinds of education in every aspect of life are to teach about positive fields to empower students to transform negative fields. For example, positive education in science and technology tries to discover, develop, and apply positive fields to help humanity live healthier and happier lives in every aspect.

I honor all healing modalities and methods, all positive scientific and technological advances, and all the positive ways humanity has created and applied to transform negative information, energy, and matter to positive information, energy, and matter in every aspect of a human being's life.

I cannot emphasize enough that the purpose of this book is to introduce the Tao Calligraphy Field. This field is created by the transformative art of Tao Calligraphy, which carries a most-positive soul over matter information system to help humanity transform every aspect of life. Tao Calligraphy, which is Source Oneness transformative art, is a portal to (a) connect with Tao Source, (b) bring a Source field to humanity and Mother Earth, and (c) make it visible and tangible for healing, transformation, wisdom, nourishment, prosperity, success, and enlightenment in every aspect of life.

I will explain Tao, Tao Calligraphy, and the power and significance of Tao Calligraphy further in the next few chapters.

What Is Tao?

THE CONCEPT OF TAO was presented by Lao Zi, the ancient sage and author of *Dao De Jing*. In *Dao De Jing*, he explains Tao as the Ultimate Creator and Source and describes Tao Normal Creation.

Tao Normal Creation

Tao Normal Creation (figure 2) is explained in the first four sentences of chapter forty-two of *Dao De Jing*:

Dao sheng yi 道生一
Tao creates One.

Lao Zi explains that Tao is the Ultimate Source. Tao creates One, which is the Oneness world, called the Wu world. Wu 無 means *emptiness*. The Wu world cannot be seen, heard, or touched. It has no yin or yang, no space or time, no image or shape.

One, the Oneness world, is called hun yuan yi qi 混元一氣. Hun yuan means *blurred*. Yi means *oneness*. Qi means *energy*. There are two kinds of energy within the hun yuan yi qi. They are mixed and not separable, because hun yuan yi qi is blurred oneness energy. The two kinds of energy are named qing qi 清氣 and zhuo qi 浊氣. Qing qi is clean, pure, light qi. Zhuo qi is disturbed, turbid, heavy qi. They remain in the hun yuan yi qi condition for eons.

yi sheng er 一生二
One creates Two.

When the time comes for qi transformation, Tao separates the two qi in hun yuan yi qi, the Oneness world or blurred emptiness world. Qing qi (light, pure, clean qi) rises to form Heaven. Zhuo qi (heavy, disturbed, turbid qi) falls to form Mother Earth. Heaven and Earth are Two, which are the Yin Yang world.

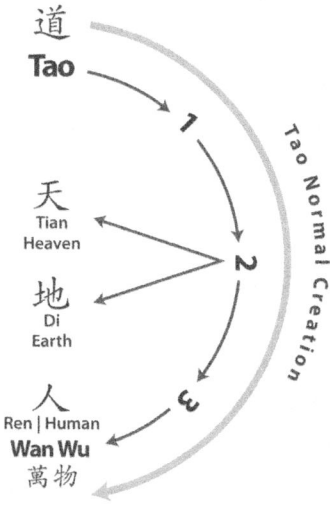

Figure 2. Tao Normal Creation

er sheng san 二生三
Two creates Three.

Hun yuan yi qi, the Oneness world, plus Heaven and Earth, which are Two or the Yin Yang world, creates Three. Oneness plus Heaven and Earth are Three.

san sheng wan wu 三生萬物
Three creates all things.

Wan means *ten thousand*, which represents *infinite, countless,* or *all*. Wu means *things*. Wan wu is *all things*. Three, which is the Oneness world plus Heaven and Earth, creates all things in countless planets, stars, galaxies, and universes.

Tao Reverse Creation

I received the teaching of Tao Reverse Creation from Tao Source. Tao Source asked me to explain Tao Reverse Creation to humanity and all souls. See figure 3.

As with Tao Normal Creation, Tao Reverse Creation is also described in four sacred sentences:

wan wu gui san 萬物归三
All things return to Three. (Gui means *to return* or *to go back*.)

san gui er 三归二
Three returns to Two.

er gui yi 二归一
Two returns to One.

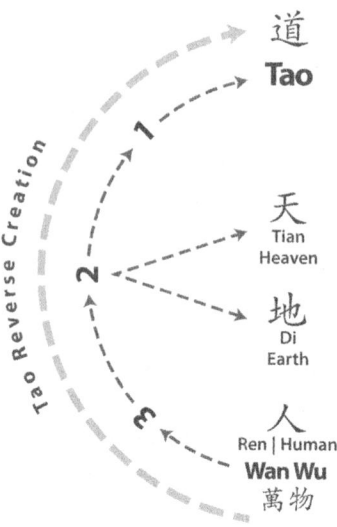

Figure 3. Tao Reverse Creation

yi gui Dao 一归道
One returns to Tao.

Together, Tao Normal Creation and Tao Reverse Creation are a universal law of universal reincarnation that explains how Tao creates One, Two, Three, and Wan Wu (all things), including countless planets, stars, galaxies, and universes, and how Wan Wu returns to Three, Two, One, and Tao, constantly and endlessly. See figure 4.

Tao Normal Creation and Tao Reverse Creation are profound. They are:

- highest wisdom
- highest philosophy

- highest science
- highest practice
- highest healing and transformation
- highest realization
- highest enlightenment
- ultimate truth

Tao Normal Creation and Tao Reverse Creation are sacred wisdom and ultimate truth that last for eons. Lao Zi was able to express Tao Normal Creation to humanity in *Dao De Jing*. It could take one decades or lifetimes to understand the profoundness and sacredness of Tao Normal Creation and Tao Reverse Creation. In one sentence:

Tao Normal Creation and Tao Reverse Creation
are the ultimate creation and reincarnation circle
for everyone and everything in countless planets,
stars, galaxies, and universes.

Figure 4. Tao Normal Creation and Tao Reverse Creation

The Ultimate Creator and Source

I would like to explain chapter one of *Dao De Jing*. Chapter one succinctly summarizes the secret wisdom and profound power of the entire *Dao De Jing*.

道可道, 非常道
Dào kě dào, fēi cháng Dào
The Tao that can be expressed in words or comprehended by thoughts is not the permanent and true Tao.

Dào is Tao, the Ultimate Source.
Kě dào means *can be explained or can be comprehended*.
Fēi means *not*.
Cháng means *permanent*.

名可名, 非常名
míng kě míng, fēi cháng míng
Anyone and anything that can be named is not permanent.

Míng means *name*.
Kě means *to be able to*.
Fēi means *not*.
Cháng means *permanent*.

Anyone who has been given a name is not permanent because the human path is sheng lao bing si 生老病死 (*birth, old age, sickness, death*). The arc of life for everyone and everything is cheng zhu huai kong 成住坏空 (*grow and develop, remain stable, be damaged and diminish, disappear*). This is the path of everyone and everything in the Yin Yang world.

无名天地之始

wú míng tiān dì zhī shǐ

The condition with no name is the beginning of Heaven and Earth.

Wú means *no*.

Míng means *name*.

Tiān means *Heaven*.

Dì means *Mother Earth*.

Zhī is a possessive particle (equivalent to *'s*).

Shǐ means *beginning*.

The condition with no name is Tao. Tao creates One, which is the Wu (emptiness) world. Tao is emptiness. Tao also creates the You (existence) world, beginning with Heaven and Earth (Two) as I explained earlier in this chapter. Mother Earth is one planet. There are countless planets, stars, galaxies, and universes. Tao Source creates all of them, as well as Heaven, Mother Earth, and human beings.

有名万物之母

yǒu míng wàn wù zhī mǔ

The ones with names are the mother of wan wu (countless things).

Yǒu means *to exist* or *to have*.

Wàn means *ten thousand*. Ten thousand in Chinese represents *infinite* or *countless* or *all*.

Wù means *thing*.

Mǔ means *mother*.

Tian and di have names: *Heaven* and *Earth*. Tian di, Heaven and Earth, are the mu qin (mother) of everyone and everything. As Lao Zi explained in Tao Normal Creation, Heaven and Earth are Two. Two creates Three. Three creates everyone and everything.

故常无, 欲以观其妙
gù cháng wú, yù yǐ guān qí miào

Therefore, be permanently in the Wu condition, which is kong (emptiness). In this condition, one can observe the profound Tao without intention, restriction, or limitation.

Gù means *therefore*.
Cháng means *permanent*.
Wú means *emptiness*, which is Tao and yi (Oneness).
Yù yǐ guān qí miào means *to be able to observe the profoundness of Tao*.

When one reaches the qing jing 清靜 (pure, quiet, and peaceful) condition in the heart, then one can go into stillness (ding 定), which means no "me, me, me" and no thoughts. In this ding condition of forgetting oneself, one could observe the profoundness and sacredness of Tao. This is a very advanced spiritual condition that is not easy to achieve.

常有, 欲以观其徼
cháng yǒu, yù yǐ guān qí jiào

Be permanently in the You condition to observe the vastness of the You world. In this condition, one can observe the You world with intention, restrictions, and limitations.

Cháng means *permanent*.
Yǒu means *existence*.
Yù means *to desire* or *to be able to*.
Guān means *to observe*.
Qí refers to *the You world*.
Jiào means *boundary*.

To see Mother Earth and countless planets, stars, galaxies,
and universes in the You world, a human's physical eyes,
consciousness, and knowledge are not enough. Using the
most advanced telescope, it still takes billions of years for
the light from the farthest stars to reach our physical eyes.
As vast as it is, the You world is limited. It has all kinds of
restrictions and limitations.

此两者, 同出而异名, 同谓之玄
cǐ liǎng zhě, tóng chū ér yì míng, tóng wèi zhī xuán
*These two (Wu and You worlds) both come from the same
source (Tao), but have different names. Both are profound.*

Cǐ means *these*.
Liǎng zhě means *two* (Wu and You worlds).
Tóng chū means *both come from Tao*.
Ér means *but*.
Yì míng means *different names*.
Tóng wèi zhī xuán means *both are profound, mysterious, sa-
cred, and unimaginable.*

玄之又玄, 众妙之门
xuán zhī yòu xuán, zhòng miào zhī mén
*The Wu and You worlds are both profound beyond profound,
mysterious beyond mysterious, sacred beyond sacred, and*

unimaginable beyond unimaginable—the gate to all sacred
teachings and realms.

Xuán means *sacredness* or *profoundness*.
Yòu is used here to indicate a deeper meaning of xuán be-
yond the literal meaning of xuán.
Zhòng means *all*.
Miào means *profound, mysterious, sacred,* or *unimaginable*.
Zhī is a possessive particle, equivalent to 's in English.
Mén means *gate*.
Zhong miao zhi men means *the gate of all sacred wisdom,*
power, and realms.

Lao Zi tried to explain Tao in many chapters of *Dao De
Jing*. Chapter one is the key to the profound wisdom and
power of Tao. Allow me to summarize the concept of Tao:

- Tao cannot be explained by words or comprehended
  by thoughts.

- Tao cannot be seen, heard, or touched.

- Tao creates the Wu world and You world, which are
  the profound gates of wisdom, philosophy, science,
  culture, practice, and power for everyone and
  everything in countless planets, stars, galaxies, and
  universes.

- Tao has no yin, no yang, no time, no space, no image,
  no shape, no sound.

- Follow Tao, flourish. Go against Tao, end.

- Tao carries the ten greatest natures, which are Da Ai
  大愛—Greatest Love, Da Kuan Shu 大宽恕—Greatest

Forgiveness, Da Ci Bei 大慈悲—Greatest Compassion, Da Guang Ming 大光明—Greatest Light, Da Qian Bei 大谦卑—Greatest Humility, Da He Xie 大和谐—Greatest Harmony, Da Chang Sheng 大昌盛—Greatest Flourishing, Da Gan En 大感恩—Greatest Gratitude, Da Fu Wu 大服务—Greatest Service, and Da Yuan Man 大圆满—Greatest Enlightenment.

- Tao expresses its ten greatest natures and powers as a Tao Source field.

- Tao carries Source most-positive information, energy, and matter (shen qi jing), which can transform negative information, energy, and matter.

- Tao is the Ultimate Creator, which is the highest soul. Therefore, Tao carries the highest soul power, which is *Tao over matter*. Tao over matter is the highest soul over matter. Soul over matter means souls can make things happen to help heal, transform, and enlighten all life. Tao over matter means Tao carries the highest power to heal, transform, and enlighten all life.

In one sentence:

Tao is The Way of all life.

What Is De?

De 德 is the shen kou yi 身口意 of Tao. This shen means *activities, actions, and behaviors*. Kou means *speech*. Yi means *thoughts*.

De is virtue, which is Source nutrients. A human receives human nutrients from fruits, vegetables, meat, and more, which carry vitamins, minerals, amino acids, proteins, and other essential nutrients.

Because de comes from Tao Source, it also carries Source nutrients, including Source liquids, vitamins, minerals, amino acids, proteins, nectars, and light. Human nutrients can be seen, tasted, touched, and felt. Source nutrients cannot be seen, tasted, touched, or felt.

Humanity has not realized enough that Tao Source nutrients are available. There is an ancient phrase that everyone should know: Dao sheng de yang 道生德养; *Tao creates, de nourishes*. The Tao Calligraphy Transformative Art Field brings Tao power with Tao Source nutrients to heal, prevent sickness, rejuvenate, nourish and prolong life, transform relationships and finances, enlighten the soul, and transform every aspect of life.

In one sentence:

De is Tao nutrients to nourish everyone and everything in countless planets, stars, galaxies, and universes.

The Power and Significance of Tao and De

Tao is the Ultimate Creator that constantly creates countless planets, stars, galaxies, and universes. Mother Earth is only one planet. Tao also creates human beings, animals, everyone, and everything. This is one of the top ancient wisdoms. It can be summarized in one sentence:

Tao creates and de nourishes countless planets, stars, galaxies, and universes, and everyone and everything, including human beings.

Tao is the universal principles and laws. Health has a Tao. Relationships have a Tao. Business and finances have a Tao. Education has a Tao. Every aspect of life has a Tao.

Tao is The Way of all life.

De, as Tao shen kou yi and Source nutrients, nourishes everyone and everything.

Tao and de exist in everyone and everything. There is an ancient philosophy and wisdom:

shun Dao chang, ni Dao wang 顺道昌, 逆道亡

This means *follow Tao, flourish; go against Tao, end* or *finish.* Everyone and everything in countless planets, stars, galaxies, and universes naturally follow this principle. Many people may not realize this.

In summary, Tao is the Ultimate Creator. De is Tao nutrients. Tao creates and de nourishes.

Tao is the universal principles and laws. Tao is The Way of all life. Tao is invisible. Lao Zi clearly explained in *Dao De Jing* that Tao cannot be seen, heard, or touched. Follow Tao, flourish. Go against Tao, end or finish.

This is to teach everyone that whether or not one realizes or believes in Tao, as the Ultimate Source it *is* guiding humanity, everyone, and everything. De as Source nutrients *is* nourishing humanity, everyone, and everything.

I have applied Tao and de wisdom and principles to create thousands of heart-touching and moving results for healing, harmonious relationships, and flourishing finances. We have completed scientific research on more than six hundred subjects to demonstrate the effectiveness and simplicity of Tao de service. (Some of our research results are presented in chapter twelve.) Tao Calligraphy Transformative Art is one of our most important tools for healing and transformation. I will explain Tao Calligraphy Transformative Art and lead you in practice so that you can experience its power and significance and receive its benefits.

Chinese Calligraphy

THE EARLIEST KNOWN written records in China date to the Shang Dynasty (1600–1046 BCE), specifically, to the reign of Emperor Wu Ding 武丁 in roughly the 13th century BCE. Records were kept in the emperor's palace through carvings on the underside of tortoise shells and on ox bones. These were also used by fortune tellers and even emperors themselves to make predictions; hence, they are also called "oracle bones." The symbols carved can be regarded as the earliest known Chinese character writing system and the mother of all subsequent Chinese script.

Chinese calligraphy is the art of writing Chinese characters. With painting, it is one of the most important ancient Chinese arts, gaining prominence and reverence during the Dong Han 东汉 (Eastern Han) Dynasty (25–220 CE).

Figure 5 below shows some of the evolution and different styles of Chinese calligraphy for six basic Chinese characters, from top to bottom: ri 日 (*sun*), yue 月 (*moon*), shan 山 (*mountain*), tian 田 (*field*), huo 火 (*fire*), and shui 水 (*water*).

Jia gu wen is the script used for oracle bones.

Figure 5. Evolution and Styles of Six Basic
Chinese Characters in Chinese Calligraphy

Jin wen ("metal script") was inscribed on ritual bronze vessels and other objects, mainly from the 13th century BCE to 770 BCE.

Xiao zhuan is the small seal script standardized by the Qin Dynasty c. 213 BCE. It is a simplified form of da zhuan, the great seal script used in the Zhou Dynasty c. 11th century BCE to 256 BCE. Da zhuan, also named zhou wen 籀 文, evolved directly from jin wen.

Li shu ("clerical script") was simplified from xiao zhuan ("small seal script") c. 200 BCE and became the official script in the Han Dynasty.

Kai shu is the "regular script" style of Chinese calligraphy, from c. 250 CE. Reaching its maturity c. 7th century CE, it is to this day the most common hanzi 汉字 (Chinese character) calligraphy script. It is also commonly used in print publications.

Xing shu is the "running script" style of Chinese calligraphy, from the 4th century CE.

Cao shu, literally "grass script," is the cursive script style of Chinese calligraphy from the 7th century CE.

Figure 6 shows these same six characters in Tao Calligraphy. I will explain Tao Calligraphy, Tao Source Oneness Transformative Art, in the next chapter.

Rì   Yuè   Shān   Tián   Huǒ   Shuǐ

Figure 6. Six Basic Chinese Characters in Tao Oneness Calligraphy

Throughout its evolution and innovation over centuries, Chinese calligraphy has been a unique visual art that always radiates charm. The techniques and the philosophy of ancient Chinese calligraphy had a strong influence on Chinese painting. The two were even melded as one in many works.

The development of Chinese characters (hanzi) over three-and-a-half millennia is a vital element of Chinese calligraphy. This artform was created and developed as an integral part of Chinese culture and honored as one of the most important and prestigious arts in the culture. Therefore, we can say that Chinese characters are one of the fundamental elements of Chinese culture.

That Chinese calligraphy is based on Chinese characters differentiates it from other calligraphies. Chinese calligraphy is an expressive art originally created during the Qin 秦 (221–207 BCE) and Han 汉 (206 BCE–220 CE) dynasties. Chinese calligraphy is praised as "poetry without language or words," "dancing without movement," "painting without a picture," and "music without sound." The historian R. Dawson has written beautifully:

The printed characters are like figures in a Victorian photograph, standing stiffly to attention; but the brush-written ones dance down the pages with the grace and vitality of the ballet. The beautiful shapes of Chinese calligraphy were in fact compared with natural beauties, and every stroke was thought to be inspired by a natural object and to have the energy of a living thing. Consequently, Chinese calligraphers sought inspiration by watching natural phenomena.

Chinese calligraphy represents the extensive wisdom, knowledge, and profound scholarship of Chinese history and culture. It has become the symbol or signature of the Chinese nation.

What Is Tao Calligraphy?

I LEARNED TAO CALLIGRAPHY from the late Professor Li Qiuyun, who taught at the University of Toronto. She was honored by the United Nations as a global authority on the Chinese language. She studied in China under Tai Shi 太师, the "supreme teacher" of the family of the last emperor of China.

Professor Li was the sole lineage holder of a unique style of Chinese calligraphy named yi bi zi 一笔字, which means *one-stroke character*. In traditional regular script (also see the kai shu examples in Figure 5 on page 54), some characters are written with twenty, even thirty or more individual strokes. In yi bi zi, every character, no matter how many individual strokes it contains, is written in one continuous stroke of the brush. Even entire phrases consisting of multiple characters can be written in one continuous stroke.

I was extremely honored to become Professor Li's only lineage holder. After I learned yi bi zi, I put Tao Source power into my yi bi zi calligraphies for healing and transformation. The Tao Source power, including Source frequency and vibration, Source love and light, and Source most-positive information, energy, and matter, transforms the yi bi zi calligraphy to Tao Calligraphy. Professor Li fully supported Tao Calligraphy and made a documentary film with me.

Now, I can explain Tao Calligraphy clearly. Tao Calligraphy is Source Oneness Transformative Art. Tao Calligraphy creates and carries a Tao Source Field. Tao exists in everyone and everything.

A Tao Calligraphy Field carries:

- the power of Tao, the Ultimate Creator and Source

- Source love and light. *Love melts all blockages. Light heals and transforms all life.*

- Source frequency and vibration, which can transform negative frequency and vibration for all life

- Source most-positive information, energy, and matter, which can transform negative information, energy, and matter for all life

- Source infinite capabilities

- Source highest power of soul over matter. *Soul can make things happen. Tao has the greatest power to make things happen.*

- a Source field to transform negative fields in all life.

Therefore, I call Tao Calligraphy "Source Oneness Transformative Art," "Tao Calligraphy Transformative Art," and more.

Tao Calligraphy Transformative Art Embodies the Ten Greatest Qualities to Transform and Enlighten Every Aspect of Life

IN THE INTRODUCTION I explained shu yi zai Dao, which means *calligraphy is used to carry Tao*. How does Tao Calligraphy do this? Tao Calligraphy Source Oneness Transformative Art carries the ten greatest qualities, which are ten Tao qualities. These ten greatest qualities can transform all life, including health, relationships, finances, and the spiritual journey.

How does Tao Calligraphy work? In one sentence:

Tao Calligraphy Transformative Art carries an Ultimate Creator and Source Field that could transform all life, including health, relationships, finances, and the spiritual journey.

Apply the Tao Calligraphy Transformative Art Field for healing the physical body.

Apply the Tao Calligraphy Transformative Art Field for healing the emotional body.

Apply the Tao Calligraphy Transformative Art Field for healing the mental body.

Apply the Tao Calligraphy Transformative Art Field for healing the spiritual body.

Apply the Tao Calligraphy Transformative Art Field for transforming all kinds of relationships.

Apply the Tao Calligraphy Transformative Art Field for transforming finances and business.

Apply the Tao Calligraphy Transformative Art Field for enlightening the spiritual journey.

Apply the Tao Calligraphy Transformative Art Field for healing, transforming, and enlightening every aspect of life.

I would like to share a heart-touching story about David Meltzer, a renowned speaker, author, and entrepreneur, and the benefits he has received from applying the Tao Calligraphy Transformative Art Field.

Please enjoy this brief video:

As David shares in the video, he has experienced great success in his life. He was a multimillionaire by the time he was thirty and became the CEO of the world's most notable sports agency, which was the inspiration and model for the movie, "Jerry Maguire."

Despite all of David's success, happiness was beyond his reach. After going through serious personal challenges, David says he learned a valuable lesson: you can't buy love or happiness.

David and I met about ten years ago through our mutual book agent, Bill Gladstone. David shared his initial response to meeting me:

I was extremely skeptical. I represented the greatest athletes, celebrities, and entertainers in the world, people who carried the spirit of excellence. It took a lot to get my attention when it came to vibration, frequency, or light. But once I met Dr. and Master Sha, I knew there was something special. There was a spirit of excellence and I wanted to be around it.

I gifted David two Tao Calligraphies and instructed him to trace them for ten minutes a day. David did this dedicatedly and his life started to change:

My life changed dramatically: my health, my relationships, my perspective, my mindset. I don't even know sometimes where the wisdom and enlightenment come from. People who have known me for years will comment as they watch the speeches and the books and TV shows and all the things that I am involved with and say, "When did you get so smart?"

Even though there is no logic or reason that would tell you that by tracing a piece of art on your wall your life would change, they work. I can tell you I don't know how it works. But I step on airplanes about two hundred days a year and I still don't know how an airplane flies, but I have faith every time I step on a plane that it's safer than driving my car home. I have faith in those calligraphies. My life has been impacted exponentially in every aspect: from health, happiness, wealth, and worthiness. What more can you ask for?

People come to me and say, "Mr. Meltzer, what can I do to change my life?" The first thing I tell them to do is to say 'thank you' before they go to bed and when they wake up. The next thing I tell them to do is to get a calligraphy from Master Sha and trace it. Both don't take very much time, and both have impacted my life more than anything else that I've ever done.

David Meltzer's original desire and request were for financial abundance. He received huge financial abundance within eighteen months of receiving and tracing the Tao Calligraphy *Dao Ye Chang Sheng* 道業昌盛 (*Tao career flourishes*) and he has continued to receive more and more. However, he also explained that he has received much more than financial abundance: improved family harmony, inspired wisdom, the ability to fulfill his greatest dream to serve humanity—all of this and more have totally transformed his life.

I wrote this book to serve you and all humanity through Tao Calligraphy. I deeply wish to see all humanity benefit from Tao Calligraphy. This is the second book in my Tao Calligraphy series. I will quickly write many more books.

Please see page 185 for subsequent books I have been guided to share with humanity in this book series.

Tao Calligraphy Source Oneness Transformative Art carries Tao natures and Tao powers. It carries the ten greatest natures and powers of Tao:

1. Da Ai 大愛—Greatest Love

2. Da Kuan Shu 大宽恕—Greatest Forgiveness

3. Da Ci Bei 大慈悲—Greatest Compassion

4. Da Guang Ming 大光明—Greatest Light

5. Da Qian Bei 大谦卑—Greatest Humility

6. Da He Xie 大和谐—Greatest Harmony

7. Da Chang Sheng 大昌盛—Greatest Flourishing

8. Da Gan En 大感恩—Greatest Gratitude

9. Da Fu Wu 大服务—Greatest Service

10. Da Yuan Man 大圆满—Greatest Enlightenment

I will explain each of these Ten Da (*greatest*) qualities in more detail.

Da Ai—Greatest Love:
Melts All Blockages and Transforms All Life

I received four sacred phrases about Da Ai, Greatest Love, from the Source:

yi shi da ai   一施大愛
wu tiao jian ai   无条件愛

rong hua zai nan 　　融化灾难
xin qing shen ming 　心清神明

一施大愛 yi shi da ai
First give greatest love to humanity and all souls
Yi means *first*. Shi means *to give*. Da means *greatest*. Ai
means *love*.

无条件愛 wu tiao jian ai
Unconditional love
Wu means *no*. Tiao jian means *condition*.

融化灾难 rong hua zai nan
Melts all disasters, hardships, and challenges
Rong hua means *to melt*. Zai nan means *disasters, hardships,
and challenges*.

心清神明 xin qing shen ming
*Heart is pure and clean and soul, heart, and mind are
enlightened*
Xin means *heart*. Qing means *pure and clean*. Shen means
soul, heart, and mind. Ming means *enlightened*.

Ancient spiritual wisdom teaches that the heart houses the
mind and soul. Physical sicknesses are due to spiritual
heart pollution, which includes greed; anger; lack of wisdom in activities, speech, and thoughts; doubt; ego; desire
for fame or money; jealousy; competition; fighting nature;
and more. These and other kinds of pollution in the spiritual heart are the true cause of sickness in the body. Millions of people are aware of this. Millions of people may not
be aware of this. Therefore, to transform physical sickness,

as well as to transform relationships and finances, one must transform one's spiritual heart. To transform the spiritual heart is to remove spiritual heart pollution, which is blockages in the spiritual heart.

Xin qing, a pure and clean heart, is a spiritual heart that has been cleansed of pollution or blockages.

Shen ming is an enlightened soul, heart, and mind.

Xin qing shen ming is first to cleanse the spiritual heart blockages. Then, enlightenment of one's soul, heart, and mind can follow.

What is enlightenment? To be enlightened is to be aware—specifically, to be aware of and to realize and embody the universal truths. Awareness is to understand that Tao Source is the Ultimate Creator that creates Heaven, Earth, and countless planets, stars, galaxies, and universes. Tao Source is The Way of all life.

Millions of people are searching for soul enlightenment, which means reaching this awareness. Millions of people may not be seeking enlightenment. People may not realize that xin qing shen ming—cleaning and purifying the spiritual heart and enlightening the soul, heart, and mind— could help one heal many sicknesses, solve many relationship and financial challenges, and make huge progress on the spiritual journey.

How can one achieve xin qing shen ming? Apply positive information, energy, and matter, which is a positive field, to transform the negative field of all kinds of spiritual heart pollution.

Tao Calligraphy creates and carries a Source field that could transform all kinds of spiritual pollution. Therefore, Tao Calligraphy could transform all life, including health, relationships, finances, and the spiritual journey, and finally help one reach soul, heart, and mind enlightenment.

In summary, the four sacred phrases about Da Ai tell us:

yi shi da ai	*First give greatest love to others and humanity*
wu tiao jian ai	*Unconditional love*
rong hua zai nan	*Melts all disasters and challenges*
xin qing shen ming	*Clean and purify the heart, enlighten the soul, heart, and mind*

Da Ai is the foundation of the Shi Da 十大. Shi means *ten*. Da means *greatest*. Shi Da or Ten Da are the ten greatest natures, qualities, and powers of Tao Source.

Da Ai is the greatest love. Greatest love is unconditional love. Greatest love is selfless love. To love unconditionally is to love without expecting anything in return. It is easy to say. It is difficult to do. But it is possible. Think about a human's life. Parents give love to their baby. Generally speaking, parents give their baby unconditional love.

To give unconditional love is to love totally from one's heart and soul, without asking for anything in return. How can you give love unconditionally to others and to humanity? The key is to reduce "me, me, me." It is very difficult for a self-centered or selfish person to give unconditional love.

Think about Heaven, Earth, the sun, and the moon. Do they ask for anything in return for their nourishment, sustenance, warmth, light, and more? They are all unconditional servants with unconditional love.

Millions of people honor Mother Mary. Millions of people honor different saints and buddhas. Mother Mary and other highest saints and buddhas carry unconditional love. They have created countless heart-touching, moving, and miraculous results through healing and transformation in every aspect of life. Therefore, Da Ai, greatest and unconditional love, carries unbelievable power to transform all life, including health, relationships, finances, and the spiritual journey.

In this book, I am further introducing a new way to carry and apply Da Ai, greatest and unconditional love. This new way is the Tao Calligraphy *Da Ai*. When I write the Tao Calligraphy *Da Ai*, I connect with Tao Source. Tao Source pours in Source love, which is the greatest love, into the calligraphy. Therefore, the *Da Ai* Tao Calligraphy carries a Source greatest love field. See figure 7.

Remember the wisdom I shared earlier: To transform any aspect of life is to apply a positive field to transform a negative field. The Tao Source highest positive field carried by Tao Calligraphy has unbelievable power to transform every aspect of life.

Figure 7. Tao Calligraphy *Da Ai* (Greatest Love)

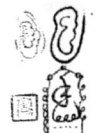

MASTER
SHA 元書
沙無畏书
二千十年十月

Hundreds of people have gathered online to experience my writing of the Tao Calligraphy *Da Ai*. As I write this Tao Calligraphy, I ask my leading teacher, Master Francisco Quintero, to do a spiritual reading:

As Master Sha prepares to write the Tao Calligraphy Da Ai, *he connects to Tao Source and many saints and buddhas in the spiritual realm. Then, as Master Sha touches his brush to the paper, each of these beings begins to pour their love and light into the Tao Calligraphy. As Master Sha continues to write, the light becomes brighter and brighter, forming a field of light that radiates in all directions. The calligraphy is transforming more and more from ordinary art to transformative art. It has become a Source healing field. The calligraphy is radiating bright golden light. The frequency and vibration are so pure. They have formed a Oneness field, carrying the unconditional love of countless saints and buddhas and the unconditional love of Tao Source.*

This Da Ai *Tao Calligraphy has such a high vibration that it instantly begins to cleanse blockages for all of us who are watching Master Sha create it. The love and light are nourishing our systems, organs, and cells, washing through the spaces and literally every cell. We are receiving a huge cleansing of our shen qi jing. This Tao Calligraphy is deeply healing and transforming all of us. It touches my heart deeply to observe these images in the spiritual realm. This calligraphy is sacred art.*

Now, I am asking everyone I have gathered online to request healing for one area of their body, which could be the physical, emotional, or mental body. You could request for a bodily system, an organ, a part of the body, or a condition. The condition could be physical, emotional, or mental, such as high blood pressure, migraines, COVID-19, depression, anger, a sore throat, shoulder pain, negative thinking, a cyst, a tumor, or cancer.

I then ask everybody to start to apply the Six Power Techniques, which are Body Power, Soul Power, Mind Power, Sound Power, Breathing Power, and Tao Calligraphy Power. I welcome you to join us in practice by following these instructions:

Apply the Six Power Techniques.

Body Power (using body and hand positions for healing)

Sit up straight. Keep your feet flat on the floor. Put one palm over your navel. Put the other palm over the area of the body where you are requesting healing and transformation. For example, for shoulder pain, place one palm on the painful shoulder.

Soul Power (soulfulness or "soul over matter" soul-healing technique, which I named Say Hello Healing and Transformation)

There are two ways to "say hello": say hello to inner souls and say hello to outer souls.

"Say hello" to inner souls:

> *Dear shen qi jing* (or soul, heart, mind, energy, and
> matter) *of my* _____ (name the system, organ,
> part of the body, or condition for which you are
> requesting healing),

I love you.
You have the power to heal yourself.
Do a great job.
Thank you.

"Say hello" to outer souls:

Dear Tao Calligraphy Transformative Art Da Ai *Field,*
I love you, honor you, and appreciate you.
You are the Tao Source most-positive field.
You can transform the negative field of my _____ (say your request again).
Please heal and transform my _____ (repeat your request).
Thank you.

Repeat the Say Hello technique to inner souls and outer souls one more time.

In fact, there is no time limit for repeating the Say Hello soul-healing technique. For decades, thousands of heart-touching stories from around the world have proven the power of the Say Hello Healing and Transformation technique. I shared two of these stories on pp. 12–14.

Breathing Power

Life is breathing in and breathing out. If one does not breathe, there is no life. It is just like the heart beating. If the heart does not beat, there is no life also.

We all know that when a person breathes in, the body receives and absorbs oxygen. When a person breathes out, the body releases and expels carbon dioxide. Oxygen is needed by every cell in the body to transform nutrients and generate energy. With every breath one takes in, the life of every cell is being nourished and sustained. Carbon dioxide is a waste product of cellular metabolism. The cells release carbon dioxide and the blood transports it to the lungs, where it is expelled with every breath out.

I am delighted to share an ancient secret breathing technique for healing and transformation. It is named "xi qing hu zhuo" 吸清呼浊.

Xi means *to breathe in*. Qing means *positive information, energy, and matter*. Hu means *to breathe out*. Zhuo means *negative information, energy, and matter*.

As I explained, everyone and everything are made of shen qi jing. Everyone's and everything's shen qi jing creates a field. The Tao Calligraphy *Da Ai* creates and carries Source shen qi jing. Therefore, the Tao Calligraphy *Da Ai* carries a Source field.

The Tao Calligraphy *Da Ai*, Greatest Love, which is unconditional love, carries immeasurable power to transform negative shen qi jing, which form a negative field. When people connect with the Tao Calligraphy *Da Ai* Field, some could feel transformation instantly. Some people could take more time to feel better.

I am continuing the live demonstration online for hundreds of people. Each one, including you, dear reader, has made a request for healing and transformation of one aspect of the physical, emotional, or mental bodies. Let us continue to practice together now.

Follow my instructions:

Breathing Power and Tao Calligraphy Power together with Mind Power (creative visualization) and Sound Power (chanting sacred messages, sounds, or mantras)

Open the book to figure 7 (page 68). Inhale deeply. As you inhale, you are receiving the positive frequency and vibration and the positive information, energy, and matter from the Tao Calligraphy *Da Ai* Field. Visualize this as golden light coming into the area where you requested healing by applying Soul Power above.

Now exhale. As you exhale, chant *Da Ai* (pronounced *dah eye*). This is Sound Power. The positive field of the Tao Calligraphy *Da Ai* will help you transform and release the negative field of your request, whether it was for relief from pain, inflammation, a cyst or tumor, cancer, or another physical sickness or disease, anger, anxiety, fear, or another emotional issue, or a mental issue such as negative thinking or poor concentration.

This is the ancient xi qing hu zhuo sacred breathing technique with the addition of Tao Calligraphy Power. We are breathing in the Tao Calligraphy *Da Ai* most-positive field and breathing out the negative field related to our request.

I am leading hundreds of people live to do this practice together for about twenty minutes. Please do it now so that you can also experience the power of the Tao Calligraphy Transformative Art Field. I always say: *If you want to know if a pear is sweet, taste it. If you want to know the power of the Tao Calligraphy Field, experience it.*

Practice

Connect with the Tao Calligraphy *Da Ai* Field in figure 7.

Breathe in. Visualize golden light bringing the Tao Calligraphy *Da Ai* Field to the area for which you requested healing and transformation.

Breathe out the negative field, which is negative information, energy, and matter, from the area of your request as you chant *Da Ai*.

Continue this practice for about twenty minutes.

Breathe in.

Breathe out ...

How do you feel?

Here are some results that participants in my live gathering reported after these twenty minutes of practice:

Renewed energy, clarity, and resolve

I am an acupuncturist in the beautiful Pacific Northwest coast in Oregon, USA, and operate a clinic that services people with chronic pain and other health conditions. I am married to my wonderful partner, Dan. My hobbies include spending time with loved ones, going for walks and hikes in nature, and doing volunteer work such as serving the homeless. I love reading, crafts, cooking, and swimming.

When I came across Master Sha's soul over matter techniques in 2015, I was blown away. I immediately started integrating them in my clinic and sharing them with some of my clients. I noticed that those clients responded much faster to the treatments I was giving them and I fell in love with this body of work.

I have been able to heal many areas of my life I never knew were possible because of the work Master Sha has so openly shared. I am a well-trained acupuncturist and expert diagnostician. I have trained with many different doctors and schools of thought when it comes to acupuncture and Chinese medicine. However, nothing could prepare me for how much more effective acupuncture is when combined with Master Sha's techniques.

Master Sha recently offered a group remote healing blessing with a Da Ai (Greatest Love) Tao Calligraphy he had just written. Prior to this, I had been feeling exhausted with some mental heaviness. After the blessing, I felt a great deal of release and lightness. The symptoms I was experiencing have dissolved and I feel renewed. This Da Ai healing blessing helped me completely turn things around and renewed my state of energy, clarity, and resolve.

I cannot express my gratitude enough for what I experienced with Tao Calligraphy Transformative Art. It is incredible that this transformed so quickly in a matter of minutes! Thank you from the bottom of my heart for this miracle healing.

— James Carter

Mind-blowing power for healing and transformation

I am married with no children, a retired multi-national business executive, now transformed to a meditation teacher, spiritual healer, and published author.

Today I joined a Tao Calligraphy Transformative Art healing event with Master Sha, who wrote a beyond-powerful Da Ai Tao Calligraphy. My eyes were very tired as it was the end of the day for me. I had a severe headache; the pain was 8–9 out of 10. I was in very deep pain, literally twisting and turning to shake off the pain. I closed my eyes and stayed in the high-frequency field of light as Master Sha offered a xi qing hu zhuo (breathing in the positive Tao Calligraphy Da Ai Field, breathing out the negative field of my headache) self-healing practice with the Da Ai Tao Calligraphy.

After the healing session, my painful headache was totally gone! The speed and power of healing and transformation Tao Calligraphy Transformative Art brings are mind-blowing!

Thank you, Master Sha, for your generosity. I am so grateful for Tao Calligraphy Transformative Art.

— E. O.

Very deep clearing transforms fear

I lived in various beach cities of Los Angeles County for many years, in San Francisco, California for five years, and then in Princeton, New Jersey. Since 2006, I have lived in Bucks County, Pennsylvania, north of Philadelphia along the Delaware River.

Lots of historic farms, stone houses, open space, and multi-family developments growing.

I've had a few different careers, including event planning and designing for trade shows and smaller events, two business partnerships, and selling and marketing of senior living communities. I am an ordained Interfaith Minister and recently certified as an end-of-life doula.

I have been on a spiritual path since I was a young child, greatly influenced by my grandmother. I practiced various meditations, EFT (Emotional Freedom Technique) with great success for several months before my divorce, and spiritual practices, including four years of deep forgiveness practices before hearing of Master Sha.

Words cannot express the peace and nourishment I received when Master Sha offered a healing blessing with the Da Ai Tao Calligraphy he had just written during an online healing event. I requested a healing blessing to transform the unbalanced emotion of fear because I have had much fear arise related to my finances.

During the meditation and breathing practice in the Da Ai Tao Calligraphy Transformative Art Field, I felt gentle radiating heat in my kidneys and up my spine to the base of my neck. I saw faint images with my spiritual channels, including lots of crystal light, and felt tiny vibrations all over my body.

After the healing session, I looked at my bank account balance and my heart was calm. No flutters in my heart or stomach like

I had been experiencing, so I know this was a very deep clearing of blockages for me. I am so grateful.

— Judy Sato

Revolutionary high-frequency healing for humanity

I am a fifty-five-year-old social media expert, consultant, trainer, speaker, and business owner. I live in Gaaden, Austria, a small town close to Vienna, with three cats named San San, Seeker Rose, and Gracie Sophie. Gracie belongs to Andrea, a good friend who lives with me. We live in the quiet countryside at the border of a national park with a forest and a lake nearby. We enjoy nature and love to exercise by walking and running in the woods after work to relax.

About four months ago, I developed liver and gallbladder issues, which started with gallbladder meridian pain that radiated to my back and all the way to the right side of my leg. My liver also became very sensitive to touch.

Due to my daily liver pain (which was typically 6–8 on a scale of 1–10), I had constant tension in my body. Moving my body was uncomfortable and the cool winter air would increase my pain when I went outside. I had pain in my lower back and down my right leg to the knee, which prevented me from exercising. While I normally enjoy walking and running, my movement was limited and I gained weight from lack of exercise. At night I could not sleep on my right side as it caused pain in my very sensitive liver. I was getting impatient and a bit frustrated with my condition. I tried to reduce the pain by changing my eating habits, but it had no effect.

I am so grateful that I had the opportunity to receive a Da Ai Tao Calligraphy Transformative Art healing blessing from Master Sha in a recent event. We did "xi qing hu zhuo" breathing-in and breathing-out practice using the field power of the Da Ai Tao Calligraphy, which Master Sha had just written. Within one hour, my pain was reduced to zero! This is incredibly powerful transformation within such a short period of time. I am so happy that I can move freely and exercise again without pain.

I cannot thank you enough, Master Sha, for bringing this revolutionary high-frequency healing to humanity.

— Natascha Ljubic

I led this practice with the Tao Calligraphy *Da Ai* Field two more times online over the next two days. After completing all three days of practice, here are some additional reports we have received.

My heart melted into absolute peace

I live in Oregon with my husband and worked in the maintenance department of a large manufacturing company. I am now retired.

I was struggling with issues causing negative emotions when Master Sha offered a blessing with his Da Ai Tao Calligraphy Transformative Art Field during a special event last week. I asked for healing of my emotional heart and felt my heart melt into a state of absolute peace.

Whatever upset me to begin with is no longer relevant. I am so grateful for this healing through Tao Calligraphy Transformative Art.

— Patricia LeClair

Unexpected benefits

I am a sixty-five-year-old male retired IT Analyst living in the San Francisco Bay Area of California. I am single with one adult daughter. I am fascinated by nature, the fine arts, and personal cultivation. I have studied many ancient traditions and am delighted to share their wisdom and practices with others. My favorite places are Mt. Shasta, Hawaii, Sedona, and Big Sur. I thrive in wild places. At the summer solstice in 2021, I held a spiritual retreat on and around Mt. Shasta.

On January 13, 2022, I received a healing blessing from Master Sha's Da Ai Tao Calligraphy that he wrote during a live webcast event. I became generally more relaxed. My thoughts calmed. I became sleepy.

What I did not expect was the relaxation and greater harmony that I experienced in my neck and jaw. I felt a hush, a silence in my body. While this may seem ordinary for many people, it has been rare for me. I am grateful to have had the opportunity to receive this wonderful blessing from the Tao Source healing field.

— Jeffrey Remis

Wonderful result for dry, painful eyes

I am sixty-six years old and live in a small town in the south-west of Germany. I have worked different jobs, mostly looking at a computer screen for many hours per day. I am divorced with no children and have three sisters and one brother.

I have very dry and painful eyes, which makes work and daily life uncomfortable, stressful, and often very difficult. Sometimes my eyes are extremely tired and I cannot read anything. My eye issue is a result of heavy medications that I took two years ago.

In an introductory Tao Calligraphy Transformative Art event several days ago, Master Sha created a new Tao Calligraphy Da Ai and generously offered a healing blessing to all participants for one issue of our choosing. He guided us through some breathing practice with the Tao Calligraphy Transformative Art Field. I requested healing for my eyes because they were very dry and painful from too much computer work.

During the healing and breathing practice, I felt soothing liquid and light coming into my eyes and they relaxed for the first time in weeks. It felt so good. After the event, I felt energy moving not only in my eyes but in my whole body. The next morning, I woke up fresh and could still feel the improvement of my eyes.

It is now nearly a week later and my eyes are tired, but not nearly as much as before the Da Ai healing blessing. They are also not nearly as dry as they were. This is a wonderful result for which I am very grateful.

I will continue to practice and participate in more Tao Calligraphy Transformative Art healing events.

Thank you.

— I. L.

The Tao Calligraphy *Da Ai* Field could transform every aspect of life beyond comprehension. Please start to use the Tao Calligraphy *Da Ai* Field in figure 7. There is no time limit. Da Ai is the greatest healer for all kinds of sickness, including sickness in the physical body, emotional body, mental body, and spiritual body. Da Ai can transform all kinds of relationships. Da Ai can transform your finances and business. Da Ai can open your heart and soul.

As you have read, I led hundreds of people online in three days of the xi qing hu zhuo breathing practice in the Tao Calligraphy *Da Ai* Field for about twenty minutes each day. This field is given to you and humanity in figure 7. I wish you to practice and receive great benefits, and then share this sacred practice with your loved ones.

For Da Ai, the first of the Ten Da greatest qualities, I close with one sentence:

Da Ai, Greatest Love, which is unconditional love, melts all blockages in every aspect of life.

Da Kuan Shu—Greatest Forgiveness:
Brings Inner Joy and Inner Peace

About six years ago, one evening when I was in Los Angeles to teach and heal, I received the Source sacred phrases for Shi Da, which means *Ten Greatest.*

The sacred phrases I received for Da Kuan Shu, Greatest Forgiveness, are:

er da kuan shu   二大宽恕
wo yuan liang ni   我原谅你
ni yuan liang wo   你原谅我
xiang ai ping an he xie   相愛平安和谐

二大宽恕 er da kuan shu
The second of the Ten Da is greatest forgiveness
Er means *second.* Da means *greatest.* Kuan shu means *forgiveness.*

我原谅你 wo yuan liang ni
I forgive you
Wo means *I.* Yuan liang means *to forgive.* Ni means *you.*

你原谅我 ni yuan liang wo
You forgive me

相愛平安和谐 xiang ai ping an he xie
Love, peace, harmony
Xiang ai means *love.* Ping an means *peace.* He xie means *harmony.*

Greatest forgiveness is unconditional forgiveness. Forgiveness is one of the highest secrets for healing. People may not realize that many sicknesses and many relationship and financial challenges are due to anger, depression, anxiety, worry, grief, fear, and other emotional and mental imbalances in one's relationships. *Forgiveness brings inner joy and inner peace.* To forgive others is to balance our emotions and bring peace to our minds. Therefore, forgiveness is one of the golden keys for healing.

Think about your family or your workplace. There may be some relationship challenges among your family members or your coworkers. You may have some relationship challenges yourself with a family member or a coworker. If family members and colleagues could truly offer unconditional forgiveness to each other, their relationship challenges with each other could be resolved quickly.

The four sacred phrases for Da Kuan Shu, Greatest Forgiveness, tell us:

er da kuan shu	*Second is greatest forgiveness*
wo yuan liang ni	*I forgive you*
ni yuan liang wo	*You forgive me*
xiang ai ping an he xie	*Love, peace, harmony*

Whenever you are upset with others or others are upset with you, if you follow these sacred phrases—*I forgive you. You forgive me. Bring love, peace, and harmony*—the upset will be gone. Unfortunately, many people cannot forgive each other. They choose to argue or fight back. There are all kinds of ways to respond negatively. I would like to share more of Lao Zi's great wisdom. In the final chapter of *Dao De Jing*, chapter eighty-one, Lao Zi teaches: "Tian zhi dao, li er bu hai; ren zhi dao, wei er bu zheng." This means *Heaven's nature and rule are to benefit and not harm others; a human's way and rule are to benefit and not fight with others.*

Suppose family member "A" and family member "B" have challenges with each other. If they continue to fight or argue, the challenges will never be resolved. They could get worse and worse. But if "A" sincerely apologizes to "B" and "B" sincerely apologizes to "A" and they forgive each other, then their relationship could quickly transform to one of love, peace, and harmony.

Millions of people believe in Jesus. When Jesus said, "You are forgiven," he was representing the Divine to forgive a person's mistakes. Then miraculous healings of blind people, lepers, paralyzed people, and more, including some distant or remote healings, happened.

What did Jesus do? He sent positive information through the message, "You are forgiven." This positive information carries Divine and Heaven's love, forgiveness, and light. It instantly transformed the person's negative information, energy, and matter, creating a miracle.

The Tao Calligraphy Field also carries positive information, energy, and matter, which could transform negative information, energy, and matter for health, relationships, finances, the spiritual journey, and every aspect of life.

To summarize in one sentence:

Da Kuan Shu, Greatest Forgiveness,
which is unconditional forgiveness, brings
love, peace, and harmony to every aspect of life.

Practice greatest forgiveness. The results could be unbelievable.

Da Ci Bei—Greatest Compassion:
Boosts Energy, Stamina, Vitality,
and Immunity, and Rejuvenates

The third Ten Da greatest quality is Da Ci Bei, Greatest Compassion. The sacred phrases I received from the Source for greatest compassion are:

san da ci bei   三大慈悲
yuan li zeng qiang   愿力增强
fu wu zhong sheng   服务众生
gong de wu liang   功德无量

三大慈悲 san da ci bei
The third greatest quality is greatest compassion
San means *third*. Da means *greatest*. Ci bei means *compassion*.

愿力增强 yuan li zeng qiang
Increase and uplift will power
Yuan li means *will power*. Zeng means *to increase*. Qiang means *strong*.

服务众生 fu wu zhong sheng

Serve humanity
Fu wu means *to serve*. Zhong sheng means *humanity*.

功德无量 gong de wu liang
Virtue is immeasurable
Gong de means *virtue*. Wu liang means *immeasurable*.

In the spiritual journey, if one gives love, care, and help to others unconditionally, Heaven records this service. Heaven then gives Heaven's flowers to this one as a reward. Heaven's flowers are named virtue. Virtue (*gong de* in Chinese) can bless every aspect of life, including for healing, harmonious relationships, flourishing finances, and enlightening the spiritual journey.

san da ci bei	*Third is greatest compassion*
yuan li zeng qiang	*Increases and uplifts will power*
fu wu zhong sheng	*Serve humanity*
gong de wu liang	*Virtue is immeasurable*

Compassion is a very important quality for any human being. Millions of people know Guan Yin, the compassion buddha. She is a universal mother known around the world. Like Jesus, she has saved countless lives miraculously. For example, in ancient times, fishermen out on the ocean would find the weather suddenly change. Huge winds howled and tidal waves capsized the fishermen's boat, throwing them into the ocean. One fisherman was sure he would drown and die, but he remembered to call Heaven: "Guan Yin, jiu ming 观音救命." Jiu means *to save*. Ming means *life*. Guan Yin jiu ming means *Guan Yin, save my life*. After making this desperate appeal, the fisherman sank into the ocean and lost consciousness. When he awoke, he was lying on the seashore. His life was saved. There are many stories like this. Therefore, in Southern China, many large statues of Guan Yin have been constructed, and many temples have been built in China and around the world to honor and commemorate Guan Yin's greatest compassion as a universal mother.

Other stories of Guan Yin's miraculous powers come from people who had stage four metastasized cancer. Medically, they had no hope. But they had reverence for and belief in Guan Yin. They chanted *Na Mo Guan Shi Yin Pusa* 南无观世音菩萨 nonstop. Na mo means *to honor*. Guan Shi Yin, Guan Yin's full name, means *she who hears the cries of humanity's suffering*. Pusa means *bodhisattva*. Many stories have been reported throughout history that these cancer sufferers and others with hopeless conditions were healed.

Guan Yin became a buddha, which is the highest awareness and enlightenment, long long ago. This is the highest achievement on one's spiritual journey. Guan Yin made the biggest vow: "If there is one sentient being who is not enlightened, I will not use the title 'buddha.'" A pusa, or bodhisattva, has reached a very high level of spiritual attainment, just below the buddha level, which is like the highest saint in other traditions. A pusa has not reached complete, highest awareness and enlightenment, but a pusa is still a high-level saint. Guan Yin calls herself a pusa because of her great humility and her biggest vow.

Today Guan Yin is a household name. Not only Buddhists, but literally millions of people around the world of many different belief systems and traditions honor Guan Yin. People deeply love her and respect her. She is truly an unconditional and selfless servant. She is the Bodhisattva of Compassion who lives in people's hearts and souls forever.

Compassion has unique power to boost energy, stamina, vitality, and immunity. Compassion rejuvenates. Compassion increases willpower. Compassion has greatest love. Compassion serves unconditionally. Therefore, Da Ci Bei, Greatest Compassion, is one of the highest qualities in the Ten Da.

In one sentence:

Da Ci Bei, Greatest Compassion, which is unconditional compassion, boosts energy, stamina, vitality, and immunity, as well as rejuvenates, in every aspect of life.

Da Guang Ming—Greatest Light: *Heals and Transforms All Life*

The sacred phrases I received for Da Guang Ming, Greatest Light, are:

si da guang ming	四大光明
wo zai Dao guang zhong	我在道光中
Dao guang zai wo zhong	道光在我中
tong ti tou ming	通体透明

四大光明 si da guang ming
The fourth of the ten greatest qualities is greatest light and transparency
Si means *fourth*. Da means *greatest*. Guang ming means *light and transparency*.

我在道光中 wo zai Dao guang zhong
I am within Tao Source light
Wo means *I*. Zai means *to be at*. Dao guang means *Tao Source light*. Zhong means *within*.

道光在我 Dao guang zai wo zhong
Tao Source light is within me
Dao guang means *Tao Source light*. Zai means *to be at*. Wo means *I*. Zhong means *within*.

通体透明 tong ti tou ming
Whole body is transparent
Tong means *whole*. Ti means *body*. Tou ming means *transparent*.

Everybody understands that when you go into a room at night, you need to turn on a light to be able to see. Scientists have shown that the human body shines all kinds of light. This light may not be visible to physical eyes. But it could be visible to special cameras or other special instruments. It could also be visible to some people who have wide-open spiritual channels.

Da Guang Ming is the greatest light from Tao Source. Tao Source light is invisible but it exists. Da Guang Ming connects with Source light. This light can transform our negative information, energy, and matter. Greatest light carries some of the most-positive information, energy, and matter, which can transform every aspect of life, including health, relationships, and finances, and enlighten one's spiritual journey.

si da guang ming	*Fourth is greatest light*
wo zai Dao guang zhong	*I am within Tao Source light*
Dao guang zai wo zhong	*Tao Source light is within me*
tong ti tou ming	*Whole body is transparent*

Imagine you are within Tao Source light. Tao Source light carries Source information, energy, and matter, which is the purest information, energy, and matter, and which can transform the negative information, energy, and matter in every aspect of life. Chanting and visualizing these four lines together is beyond powerful. The benefits could be remarkable beyond comprehension.

In one sentence:

**Da Guang Ming, Greatest Light,
heals and transforms every aspect of life.**

Da Qian Bei—Greatest Humility:
Prevents and Heals Ego in Order to Grow Persistently

I received the following sacred phrases for Da Qian Bei, Greatest Humility, from the Source:

wu da qian bei	五大谦卑
rou ruo bu zheng	柔弱不争

chi xu jing jin   持续精进
shi qian bei   失谦卑
die wan zhang   跌万丈

五大谦卑 wu da qian bei
The fifth of the ten greatest qualities is greatest humility
Wu means *fifth*. Da means *greatest*. Qian bei means *humility*.

柔弱不争 rou ruo bu zheng
Be soft, gentle, and weak; do not fight, strive, or argue
Rou means *soft and gentle*. Ruo means *weak*. Bu zheng
means *not to fight, strive, or argue.*

There is a famous statement: di shui chuan shi 滴水穿石,
which means *dripping water can pierce through a rock*. Kong
Zi, known as Confucius, the founder of Confucianism,
met Lao Zi, the author of *Dao De Jing*. One of Lao Zi's major teachings is rou ruo sheng gang qiang 柔弱胜刚强 (*soft
and weak can overcome hard and firm*). Lao Zi opened his
mouth to show Kong Zi his tongue and missing teeth and
asked, "Who stays longer? The teeth or the tongue?" The
tongue is soft but stays much longer than the hard teeth.

持续精进 chi xu jing jin
Continue to forge ahead vigorously in every aspect of life.
Chi xu means *to continue*. Jing jin means *to forge ahead vig-
orously.*

失谦卑 shi qian bei
Lose humility
Shi means *to lose*. Qian bei means *humility*.

跌萬丈 die wan zhang
Fall infinitely deep
Die means *to fall*. Wan means *ten thousand*, which represents *infinite* or *countless* in Chinese. Zhang is a unit of length, *approximately 3.3 meters*.

Wang Yang Ming was a renowned philosopher and calligrapher in early sixteenth century China. One of his most famous teachings is xin xue 心学, which means *heart study*. He also taught, "Ego is the biggest enemy for life." Da Qian Bei, Greatest Humility, is the key to heal ego and prevent ego from developing. Ego can block every aspect of life, including health, relationships, business, finances, and the spiritual journey. Ego could cause one to make huge mistakes. To transform ego is very important to transform all life.

In chapter nine of *Dao De Jing*, Lao Zi wrote: fu gui er jiao, zi yi qi jiu 富贵而骄, 自遗其咎. *Wealth, rank, and pride will bring one disasters.*

wu da qian bei	*Fifth is greatest humility*
rou ruo bu zheng	*Gentle, soft, and weak; do not fight, strive, or argue*
chi xu jing jin	*Continuously move forward with vigor*
shi qian bei	*Lose humility*
die wan zhang	*Fall infinitely deep*

Tao is Greatest Humility. Tao creates everyone and everything. Tao nourishes everyone and everything. Tao does not take credit for anyone or anything. Tao is beyond powerful. Tao is gentle and soft. Tao is unheard, unseen, unfelt. Tao gives us free will. Tao does not interfere, fight, strive, or argue. If we simply connect with Tao through the Tao Calligraphy Field and ask Tao for a blessing, Tao blesses us unconditionally. Therefore, Tao is Greatest Humility.

In one sentence:

Da Qian Bei, Greatest Humility,
prevents and heals ego in every aspect of life.

Da He Xie—Greatest Harmony:
The Secret of Success

I received four sacred phrases for Da He Xie, Greatest Harmony:

liu da he xie	六大和谐
san ren tong xin	三人同心
qi li duan jin	其利断金
cheng gong mi jue	成功秘诀

六大和谐 liu da he xie
The sixth of the ten greatest qualities is greatest harmony
Liu means *sixth*. Da means *greatest*. He xie means *harmony*.

三人同心 san ren tong xin
Three people who join hearts together
San means *three*. Ren means *person*. Tong means *to join together*. Xin means *heart*.

其利断金 qi li duan jin
Their strength is like a sharp sword that can cut through gold

Qi refers to *the three people who join hearts together*. Li means *sharp*. Duan means *cut*. Jin means *gold*.

成功秘诀 cheng gong mi jue
The secret of success
Cheng gong means *success*. Mi jue means *secret*.

Three major philosophies and teachings are at the core of Chinese culture: Taoism, Buddhism, and Confucianism. For example, the theory of traditional Chinese medicine comes from Tao teachings.

He xie, which is harmony, is a key teaching in Taoism, Buddhism, Confucianism, and traditional Chinese medicine. For example, a human being has a liver, heart, spleen, lungs, kidneys, brain, and various other organs. Harmony among all of them is the key for health.

Every family needs harmony. There is an ancient statement: jia he wan shi xing 家和萬事興. Jia means *family*. He means *harmonious*. Wan means *ten thousand*, which represents *countless* or *all*. Shi means *thing*. Xing means *to flourish*. Jia he wan shi xing means *a harmonious family brings flourishing to everything*.

Every business and every organization need harmony. Harmony is the vital secret for health, relationships, and success in every aspect of life.

For example, for a business to have success, two teams are needed: the physical team and a Heaven's team. When there is harmony within the physical team, each department and division have harmony with every other department and division, and all the employees have harmony not only with each other but also with many qualities of the business, such as the strategic vision, implementation plans, controls, marketing, and much more. Harmony is the key.

The secret wisdom for success in a person, a family, an organization, a business, a society, a city, a country, Mother Earth, and countless planets, stars, galaxies, and universes is harmony.

liu da he xie	*Sixth is greatest harmony*
san ren tong xin	*Three people who join hearts together*
qi li duan jin	*Their sharpness can cut through gold*
cheng gong mi jue	*The profound secret and key to success*

There is an ancient wisdom: tian ren he yi 天人合一. Tian means *the bigger universe, which is Heaven's team.* Ren is *the smaller universe, which is a human being's team.* He means *to join as.* Yi means *oneness.* Tian ren he yi means *Heaven's team and a human being's team join as one in greatest harmony.* This is the greatest secret for greatest success.

In one sentence:

Da He Xie, Greatest Harmony,
is the key to success in every aspect of life.

Da Chang Sheng—Greatest Flourishing:
The Engine for Further Achievement

I received these sacred phrases for Da Chang Sheng, Greatest Flourishing:

qi da chang sheng	七大昌盛
Dao ci ying fu	道赐盈福
xing shan ji de	行善积德
Dao ye chang sheng	道業昌盛

七大昌盛 qi da chang sheng
The seventh of the ten greatest qualities is greatest flourishing
Qi means *seventh*. Da means *greatest*. Chang sheng means *flourishing* or *prosperous*.

道赐盈福 Dao ci ying fu
Tao Source bestows huge blessings and good fortune in any aspect of life
Dao is Tao Source. Ci means *to bestow*. Ying fu means *huge blessings and good fortune in any aspect of life*.

行善积德 xing shan ji de
Do kind things to accumulate virtue
Xing means *to act and do*. Shan means *kindness*. Ji means *to accumulate*. De means *virtue*.

道業昌盛 Dao ye chang sheng
Tao career flourishes
Dao is Tao Source. Ye means *career*. Chang sheng means *flourishing* or *prosperous*.

Tao is the Ultimate Creator which creates everyone and everything, including human beings. Tao is within everyone and everything. Every human being has Tao natures and qualities. Human beings' spiritual pollution, including greed; anger; lack of wisdom in activities, actions, behaviors, speech, and thoughts; doubt; ego; and more, blocks our health, relationships, finances, and spiritual journey. For flourishing in every aspect of life, everyone needs to communicate with Tao.

You may not think you know how to communicate with Tao. Tao is The Way of all life. When you follow Tao principles in any aspect of life, including sleeping, eating, raising children, studying, working, conducting business, and more, you *are* communicating with Tao. Then, Tao can bestow huge wisdom and success in every aspect of life.

Tao creates and nourishes everyone and everything. If you serve unconditionally, you will receive much more than someone who does not serve unconditionally. Only through unconditional service can your career be very flourishing. If you serve others, you are following Tao principles. Therefore, your career is a Tao career. If you serve others selfishly, your career is not a Tao career.

The more you apply Ten Da in your occupation or profession, the more your work could flourish. The more you apply Ten Da in your daily life, the more every aspect of your life could flourish.

qi da chang sheng	*Seventh is greatest flourishing*
Dao ci ying fu	*Tao Source bestows huge blessing and fortune*
xing shan ji de	*Do kind things to accumulate virtue*
Dao ye chang sheng	*Tao career flourishes*

Tao creates Heaven, Mother Earth, and countless planets, stars, galaxies, and universes, including human beings. Tao and de nourish everyone and everything. Tao ci ying fu means *Tao bestows huge blessing and fortune in every aspect of life.* These four sacred phrases for Da Chang Sheng teach the secret that if everyone truly connects with Tao, Tao could bestow huge blessing and fortune.

In one sentence:

Da Chang Sheng, Greatest Flourishing, is the energy and support to serve more in every aspect of life.

Da Gan En—Greatest Gratitude:
The Key for Progress

I received these sacred phrases for Da Gan En, Greatest Gratitude:

ba da gan en	八大感恩
Dao sheng de yang	道生德养
zai pei ci hui	栽培赐慧
Dao en yong cun	道恩永存

八大感恩 ba da gan en
The eighth of the Ten Da qualities is greatest gratitude

Ba means *eighth*. Da means *greatest*. Gan en means *gratitude*.

道生德养 Dao sheng de yang
Tao Source creates and de nourishes
Sheng means *creates*. De is the *shen kou yi* (actions, activities, behaviors, speech, thoughts) *and virtue of Tao*. Yang means *nourishes*.

栽培赐慧 zai pei ci hui
Tao Source cultivates and bestows wisdom and intelligence to everyone and everything
Zai pei means *to cultivate, grow, and educate*. Ci means *to bestow*. Hui means *wisdom*.

道恩永存 Dao en yong cun
Our honor of Tao will last forever
En means *honor*. Yong cun means *to exist forever*.

Greatest gratitude is one of the highest qualities we could have. Think about our parents who raised us. Think about our teachers in school—elementary school, high school, and college. Think about our teachers in our occupation or profession. Think about everyone who has nurtured our wisdom, knowledge, love, compassion, and more. Think of those who have been examples for us of how to act and speak. Think of those who corrected our mistakes. Without all of them, we would not have been able to grow into who we are. We need to have gratitude to everyone who has helped us in our life. We also need to have gratitude for the lessons we have learned in life. The lessons we learn make us wiser so that we will not make the same mistakes again.

ba da gan en	*Eighth is greatest gratitude*
Dao sheng de yang	*Tao creates, de nourishes*
zai pei ci hui	*Tao bestows wisdom to all*
Dao en yong cun	*Our honor of Tao will remain forever*

Anyone who holds the greatest gratitude will progress in every aspect of life. Gratitude should come from the heart and soul. Gratitude is so important for life.

Tao Source creates us, nourishes us, and bestows wisdom and grace to us to empower us to succeed in every aspect of life. We cannot express enough the greatest gratitude to Tao and de. Therefore, our honor for the favor, blessings, and grace of Tao and de should always remain in our hearts and souls.

In one sentence:

Da Gan En, Greatest Gratitude, is the key for accelerating success in every aspect of life.

Da Fu Wu—Greatest Service:
The Purpose of Life

The sacred phrases I received for Da Fu Wu, Greatest Service, are:

jiu da fu wu	九大服务
shi wei gong pu	誓为公仆
wu si feng xian	无私奉献
shang cheng fa men	上乘法门

九大服务 jiu da fu wu
The ninth of the Ten Da is greatest service
Jiu means *ninth*. Da means *greatest*. Fu wu means *service*.

誓为公仆 shi wei gong pu
Vow to be a servant of humanity
Shi means *to vow*. Wei means *to be*. Gong pu means *servant of humanity*.

无私奉献 wu si feng xian
Selflessly dedicate yourself to serve others
Wu means *not*. Si means *self*. Feng xian means *to offer to others dedicatedly and devotedly*.

上乘法门 shang cheng fa men
The highest method and gate to healing, transformation, and enlightenment of one's soul, heart, mind, and body
Shang cheng means *highest*. Fa means *dharma*. Men means *gate* or *door*.

The purpose of life is to serve. I have committed my life to this purpose. To serve is to make others happier and healthier. To serve is to empower and enlighten others.

A human being has a physical life and a spiritual journey. The physical life is limited. The spiritual journey is eternal. Physical life is given to us so that we can serve our spiritual journey, which is our soul's life.

There are two kinds of services and benefits. One kind is to serve yourself to achieve your own success and enlightenment. The other kind is to serve others to help make others successful and enlightened. Many people think to serve oneself is the priority. In fact, to serve, empower, and enlighten others is much more important.

Why does a person suffer? High-level spiritual wisdom explains that a person suffers due to self-attachment or self-centeredness. A person could turn everything they think about into thinking about themselves. This could manifest as greed; anger; lack of wisdom in what they do, what they speak, and what they think; doubt; ego; competition; jealousy, a fighting nature; and more. I have explained these earlier. I emphasize again: These qualities of self-attachment and self-centeredness are all spiritual pollution in the heart and soul. These natures of self-attachment are the root cause of all challenges in health, relationships, finances, and the spiritual journey.

To transform health, relationships, finances, and the spiritual journey, the key is less "me, me, me," less self-centeredness, and less self-attachment. A highly-enlightened spiritual being could reach the condition of completely removing "me, me, me." If one can serve others unconditionally and selflessly, every aspect of life could be transformed beyond words. I am delighted to share a one-sentence secret:

To serve others is to reduce "me, me, me"; to serve others unconditionally is to reach no "me, me, me."

Guan Yin, the Compassion Buddha, served humanity and all souls unconditionally for millions of lifetimes. Therefore, she has become a universal mother. Heaven and Tao gave her the honorable title of Qian Shou Qian Yan (*Thousand Hands, Thousand Eyes*) Da Ci Da Bei (*Greatest Compassion*) Jiu Ku Jiu Nan (*Saving Humans from Bitterness and Disasters*) Guang Da Yuan Man (*Greatest Enlightenment*) Buddha.

If you commit to serve others unconditionally, others may not become enlightened, but you could become enlightened first.

To enlighten your soul, serving unconditionally is a *must*. What does it mean to serve unconditionally? To serve unconditionally is to serve without "me, me, me." One needs to serve selflessly, without "me, me, me."

Shen kou yi is our daily life. Shen means *activities, actions, and behaviors*. Kou means *speech*. Yi means *thoughts*. Every day, everyone has shen kou yi. Can we focus our shen kou yi on serving others unconditionally? Selflessly? If so, you could receive remarkable transformation in your health, relationships, and finances, and receive unimaginable upliftment for your soul enlightenment journey.

jiu da fu wu	*Ninth of the Ten Da qualities is Greatest Service*
shi wei gong pu	*Vow to serve humanity*
wu si feng xian	*Selflessly devote yourself to serve others*
shang cheng fa men	*The highest method and gate to enlightenment*

There is a universal law called the Universal Law of Universal Service. It begins with these three statements:

**Serve others a little,
receive a little reward from Tao Source.**

**Serve others more,
receive more reward from Tao Source.**

**Serve others unconditionally,
receive unlimited reward from Tao Source.**

It does not matter who you are. It does not matter what job you are doing. In what you do, in what you speak, and in what you think, always remember to make others healthier, happier, empowered, and enlightened.

Humanity has all kinds of challenges, including in health, relationships, finances, and the spiritual journey. The absolute key for service is selfless service or unconditional service to others, without "me, me, me." It is easy to say but very difficult to do.

Therefore, Da Fu Wu, greatest, unconditional, and selfless service, carries Tao information, energy, and matter, which can transform our negative information, energy, and matter so that we can serve others unconditionally and selflessly.

In one sentence:

**Da Fu Wu, Greatest Service,
is the purpose of life in every aspect.**

Da Yuan Man—Greatest Enlightenment:
The Ultimate Achievement for One's Life

Tao Source gave me four sacred phrases for Da Yuan Man, Greatest Enlightenment:

shi da yuan man	十大圆满
ling xin nao shen yuan man	靈心脑身圆满
ren di tian Dao shen xian ti	人地天道神仙梯
fu wu xiu lian cai ke pan	服务修炼才可攀

十大圆满 shi da yuan man
The tenth of the Ten Da qualities is Greatest Enlightenment
Shi means *tenth*. Da means *greatest*. Yuan man means *enlightenment*.

靈心脑身圆满 ling xin nao shen yuan man
Soul, heart, mind, and body enlightenment
Ling means *soul*. Xin means *heart*, which is the core of life. (This is the spiritual heart, which is the receiver of the information or messages from the soul. A human has a heart. A pet has a heart. Does a mountain have a heart? Does an ocean have a heart? Does Mother Earth have a heart? The answers are "yes." Living things have hearts. Inanimate things also have hearts.) Nao means *consciousness*. Shen means *body*. For the enlightenment journey, enlighten the soul first. Then, enlighten the heart. Next, enlighten the mind. Finally, enlighten the body.

人地天道神仙梯 ren di tian Dao shen xian ti
Saints have four major levels or steps: human saint, Mother Earth saint, Heaven saint, and Tao saint

Ren means *human being*. Di means *Mother Earth*. Tian means *Heaven*.

Dao is Tao Source. Shen xian means *saints*. Ti means *stairs*.

What is a saint? A saint has reached awareness. Awareness means to realize the universal truths and to embody the universal truths. Ten Da is the highest universal truth. Ten Da is Tao Source nature. Awareness has layers. Therefore, there are four major layers of saints.

Ren xian 人仙 means *human saint*. A ren xian can transform a human being's conditions. Human saints have also reached the fan lao huan tong 返老还童 condition. Fan means *to return*. Lao means *old age*. Huan also means *to return* or *to go back to*. Tong means *the baby state*. Fan lao huan tong means *return from old age to the purity and health of the baby state*. It is true rejuvenation.

Di xian 地仙 means *Mother Earth saint*. The quality of a di xian is very high. A di xian can transform Mother Earth's conditions.

Tian xian 天仙 means *Heaven saint*. A tian xian has even higher abilities that can transform Heaven's conditions.

Dao xian 道仙 is a *Tao Source saint*, the highest saint. A Dao xian can transform countless planets, stars, galaxies, and universes, because Tao is the Ultimate Creator and Source of countless planets, stars, galaxies, and universes.

The wisdom of the four layers of saints (ren xian, di xian, tian xian, Dao xian) is ancient secret Tao wisdom. What are the power and significance of being a ren xian, di xian, tian xian, or Dao xian? How do the saints climb the stairs to reach higher and higher layers? I have shared more profound ancient wisdom and secret practices in three books I have written on Tao.[4] If you are inspired to learn more about this advanced soul achievement, please read and practice with them.

服务修炼才可攀 fu wu xiu lian cai ke pan
Serving unconditionally is the only way to climb Heaven's and Tao's stairs to become a ren xian, di xian, tian xian, and Dao xian
Fu wu means *service*. Xiu means *purification*. Lian means *practice*. Xiu lian means *purification practice*. Fu wu xiu lian is *service purification practice*, which is to serve unconditionally. There are many spiritual belief systems. Each spiritual belief system teaches and does xiu lian in their own way. The essence is the same. Cai means *only*. Ke means *to be able*. Pan means *to climb*.

Xiu lian can be explained in one sentence:

Xiu lian is to purify a human's shen kou yi, including activities, actions, behaviors, speech, and thoughts, to a saint's shen kou yi.

---

[4] Zhi Gang Sha, *Tao I: The Way of All Life* (New York, New York/Toronto, Ontario: Atria Books/Heaven's Library Pub. Corp., 2010); *Tao II: The Way of Healing, Rejuvenation, Longevity, and Immortality* (New York, New York/Toronto, Ontario: Atria Books/Heaven's Library Pub. Corp., 2010); *Tao Classic of Longevity and Immortality: Sacred Wisdom and Practical Techniques* (Dallas, Texas/Richmond Hill, Ontario: BenBella Books/Heaven's Library Pub. Corp., 2018).

What is a human's shen kou yi? Human shen kou yi comes from self-attachment and self-centeredness. In every aspect of life, this is to consider "me, me, me" first. The purpose of xiu lian is to purify selfishness to selflessness. I cannot emphasize enough that to truly purify is to remove all kinds of human pollution, including:

- tan 贪 *greed*
- chen 嗔 *anger*
- chi 痴 *lack of wisdom in shen kou yi*
- yi 疑 *doubt*
- man 慢 *ego*
- ming 名 *fame*
- li 利 *focus on money and power*
- zheng dou 争斗 *fighting*
- du ji 妒忌 *jealousy*
- jing zheng 竞争 *competition*
- and more

Remove the above human pollution in order to reach a saint's level. Purify further and serve unconditionally to reach higher and higher layers of enlightenment.

shi da yuan man	*The tenth of the Ten Da qualities is Greatest Enlightenment*
ling xin nao shen yuan man	*Soul, heart, mind, and body enlightenment*

ren di tian Dao shen xian ti   *Saints have four major levels*
                                     or steps: human saint,
                                     Mother Earth saint, Heaven
                                     saint, and Tao saint
fu wu xiu lian cai ke pan   *Unconditional service is the*
                                     only way to climb Heaven's
                                     and Tao's stairs

In one sentence:

Da Yuan Man, Greatest Enlightenment,
is the ultimate goal and achievement of
one's spiritual journey and physical journey.

ಙ ಜಿ ಲ

Shi Da, the ten greatest qualities, is Tao Source nature, as well as Source wisdom and power to transform every aspect of life, including health, relationships, finances, and the spiritual journey.

Tao Calligraphy carries a Source field, which includes Source love and light; Source frequency and vibration; Source most-positive information, energy, and matter; Source unlimited capabilities; and Source highest power of soul over matter, which could transform negative information, energy, and matter in every aspect of life.

In the next chapter I will guide you to apply the Tao Calligraphy *Da Ai* Field to transform every aspect of life.

Tao Calligraphy Field Transformation

I WOULD LIKE to emphasize again that Tao:

- is the Ultimate Creator and Source
- carries Source love and light
- carries Source frequency and vibration
- carries Source most-positive information, energy, and matter that could transform every aspect of life, including health, relationships, finances, and the spiritual journey
- carries Source infinite abilities
- is the highest soul that carries the highest power of soul over matter. Soul over matter is soulfulness, which means soul can make things happen. Because Tao is the Ultimate Creator and Source, it has the highest soul power to transform every aspect of life.

Calligraphy is art.

Tao Calligraphy is Source Oneness art that creates and carries a Tao Source Field as a physical presence of Tao on Mother Earth. In chapter twelve, Dr. Peter Hudoba will share some key findings of medical research he has conducted on the effects of the Tao Calligraphy Transformative Art Field on subjects with depression or anxiety to help you clearly understand the power of the Tao Calligraphy Field for transforming health conditions.

Tao Calligraphy *Da Ai* Field

In the previous chapter, I shared the Tao Calligraphy *Da Ai* Field I created in figure 7 (page 68). I asked you to practice with this field for twenty minutes to serve one request. In this chapter, I will guide you to apply the Tao Calligraphy *Da Ai* Field to transform health, relationships, finances, and the spiritual journey.

Tao Calligraphy *Da Ai* Field
Transforms Health for the Physical Body

Let us apply the Six Power Techniques.

Body Power

Body Power is to use body and hand positions for healing.

Sit up straight with your back free and clear and your feet flat on the floor. Put one palm over your navel and the other palm over any part of your body where you wish to receive healing, transformation, prevention, or rejuvenation.

Soul Power

Soul Power is to apply soul over matter or soulfulness by invoking inner souls within our body and outer souls outside our body. I gave Soul Power the name "Say Hello Healing and Transformation" more than fifteen years ago.

"Say hello" to inner souls:

> *Dear soul, heart, mind, and body (or shen qi jing) of my*
> _____ (name the system, organ, part or area of
> the body, or physical health condition for which
> you wish healing[5]),
> *I love you, honor you, and appreciate you.*
> *You have the power to heal yourself.*
> *Do a great job.*
> *Thank you.*

"Say hello" to outer souls:

> *Dear the Tao Calligraphy Da Ai Field,*
> *Dear Tao Source,*
> *Dear Divine,*
> *Dear all my spiritual fathers and mothers, angels, guides,*
> *and protectors,*
> *I love you, honor you, and appreciate you.*
> *Please give me a healing for my* _____ (repeat your
> request).

---

[5] Some examples: my heart, my respiratory system, my knees, my lower back, my hypertension, my breast cancer, my migraines, etc. Any physical system, organ, part or area of the body, pain, cyst, tumor, sickness, or physical condition is fine.

I am very grateful.
Thank you.

If you want to request prevention of sickness or rejuvenation, simply replace (or add) those words for "a healing."

Breathing Power, Mind Power, Sound Power, and Tao Calligraphy Field Power

Breathing Power, Mind Power, Sound Power, and Tao Calligraphy Field Power are the remaining four of the Six Power Techniques.

For Breathing Power, we will use the ancient secret breathing practice named xi qing hu zhuo 吸清呼浊 that I introduced in the previous chapter (page 72). Remember that xi qing means *inhale positive shen qi jing* and hu zhuo means *exhale negative shen qi jing*. We all know life is breathing in and breathing out. Breathe in oxygen and breathe out carbon dioxide.

We combine the Xi Qing Hu Zhuo Breathing Power technique with Tao Calligraphy Field Power. This breakthrough synergy is much more powerful than the ancient breathing practice alone because the Tao Calligraphy Field is a Source most-positive shen qi jing field (information-energy-matter field).

Xi qing is to breathe in the positive information, energy, and matter of the *Da Ai* Tao Calligraphy Field. Have the *Da Ai* Tao Calligraphy Field in figure 7 in front of you as you do the practices in this chapter that use it.

Now, combine Breathing Power and Tao Calligraphy Field Power with Mind Power.

As you inhale deeply and slowly, visualize golden light from the *Da Ai* Tao Calligraphy Field coming to and gathering in the part or area of the physical body for which you requested healing. This golden light carries the most-positive information, energy, and matter of the Tao Calligraphy *Da Ai* Field.

Finally, add Sound Power.

As you exhale, chant *Da Ai* (pronounced *dah eye*) and visualize the golden light radiating in all directions from the area for which you requested healing, filling your whole body as you exhale negative information, energy, and matter from your request.

Continue to practice. It is best to practice for at least ten to twenty minutes per time, and you can practice several times per day. In fact, there is no time limit for this practice. For chronic pain and life-threatening conditions, practice for a total of one to two hours a day. The benefits could be beyond your comprehension.

Tao Calligraphy *Da Ai* Field
Transforms Health for the Emotional Body

Everyone can use healing, transformation, prevention, and rejuvenation for the physical body. Therefore, study the preceding section, practice well, and, most important, do it!

To use the Six Power Techniques to transform the health of the emotional body, which is to reduce, remove, and prevent unbalanced emotions, simply modify the Mind Power used in the previous practice (transforming health for the physical body) as follows:

For anger, visualize the golden light gathering in and around the liver as you inhale and radiating in all directions from your liver as you exhale, releasing negative shen qi jing.

For anxiety or depression, visualize the golden light gathering in and around your heart.

For worry, visualize the golden light gathering in and around your spleen.

For sadness or grief, visualize the golden light gathering in and around your lungs.

For fear, visualize the golden light gathering in and around your kidneys.

For other unbalanced emotions, such as guilt or shame, visualize the golden light gathering in and around your heart.

These guidelines are based on the Five Elements theory of traditional Chinese medicine. I will explain a little more about the Five Elements theory later in this chapter.

Tao Calligraphy *Da Ai* Field
Transforms Health for the Mental Body

For the mental body, you may wish healing, transformation, or prevention for issues such as negative attitudes, negative mind-sets, negative beliefs, ego, attachments, or any other mental condition.

Follow the pattern of the practice for the physical body earlier in this chapter. For Mind Power, visualize golden light from the *Da Ai* Tao Calligraphy Field coming to both the heart and the brain together. The heart houses the mind and soul.

Tao Calligraphy *Da Ai* Field
Transforms Health for the Spiritual Body

To transform health for the spiritual body is to transform negative information, energy, and matter blocking one's spiritual journey. This could include issues such as lack of belief, lack of trust, doubt, lack of discipline, resistance of all kinds, and more.

Follow the pattern of the practice for the physical body earlier in this chapter. For Mind Power, visualize golden light from the *Da Ai* Tao Calligraphy Field coming to the heart.

In this and the earlier practices, practice at least ten minutes per time, two or three times a day. For chronic or life-threatening conditions, practice for a total of two hours a day. In fact, there is no time limit. I cannot emphasize enough that life is breathing in and breathing out. You can practice for many hours a day, especially if you have a serious or life-threatening condition. Each time you practice, keep the book open to figure 7 on page 68.

Patience and persistence are important. We have had thousands of heart-touching and moving results worldwide. I wish each of you to receive the greatest benefits you can.

Practice. Practice. Practice.
Heal. Heal. Heal.
Transform. Transform. Transform.
Restore your health as soon as possible.

Tao Calligraphy *Da Ai* Field Transforms Relationships

The Tao Calligraphy Transformative Art Field is a Source Field, which is a quantum field with unlimited positive information, energy, and matter and unlimited potential. That is why the Tao Calligraphy Field can heal and transform any aspect of life, including relationships.

Few people have only perfect relationships full of love, peace, and harmony. Most people could have one or several challenging relationships. Some people have huge challenges in relationships.

Apply the Six Power Techniques to transform negative information, energy, and matter in one or more relationships.

Body Power

Sit up straight with your back free and clear and your feet flat on the floor. You may also stand up straight with your feet shoulder-width apart. Put one palm over your navel and the other palm over your first energy chakra (root chakra) at the bottom of your torso. The first energy chakra is important for relationships. See figure 9 on page 126 for the location of the first energy chakra.

Soul Power

"Say hello" to inner souls:

> *Dear soul, heart, mind, and body* (or *shen qi jing*) *of my relationship with* _____ (name the person or persons),
> *I love you, honor you, and appreciate you.*
> *You have the power to heal and transform yourself.*
> *Do a great job.*
> *Thank you.*

"Say hello" to outer souls:

> *Dear* _____ (name the person or persons),
> *I love you, honor you, and appreciate you.*
> *We have some challenges in our relationship.*
> *We have the power to heal and transform our relationship.*
> *I forgive you.*
> *You forgive me.*
> *Bring love, peace, and harmony.*

Dear the Tao Calligraphy Da Ai *Field,*
Dear Tao Source,
Dear Divine,
Dear all our (your and the other person's) *spiritual*
*   fathers and mothers, angels, guides, and protectors,*
I love you, honor you, and appreciate you.
Please give us a blessing to heal and transform my
*   relationship with* _____ (name the person or
    persons again).
I am very grateful.
Thank you.

Breathing Power, Mind Power, Sound Power, and Tao Calligraphy Field Power

Use the Xi Qing Hu Zhuo (Inhale Positive, Exhale Negative) Breathing Power technique. Open the book to figure 7 and breathe in the positive information, energy, and matter of the *Da Ai* Tao Calligraphy Field. As you inhale, visualize golden light from the *Da Ai* Tao Calligraphy Field coming to and gathering in your first energy chakra.

As you exhale, chant *Da Ai* and visualize the golden light radiating in all directions from your first energy chakra, filling your whole body as you exhale negative information, energy, and matter from your relationship.

Continue to practice for at least ten minutes per time. You can practice several times per day. In fact, there is no time limit for this practice.

Tao Calligraphy *Da Ai* Field
Transforms Finances

Apply the Six Power Techniques to transform negative information, energy, and matter in your finances.

Body Power

Sit up straight with your back free and clear and your feet flat on the floor. You may also stand up straight with your feet shoulder-width apart. Put one palm over your navel and the other palm just below, over your second energy chakra in your lower abdomen. The second energy chakra is important for finances. See figure 9 on page 126 for the location of the second energy chakra.

Soul Power

"Say hello" to inner souls:

> *Dear soul, heart, mind, and body* (or *shen qi jing*) *of my finances,*
> *I love you, honor you, and appreciate you.*
> *You have the power to heal and transform yourself.*
> *Do a great job.*
> *Thank you.*

"Say hello" to outer souls:

> *Dear the Tao Calligraphy* Da Ai *Field,*
> *Dear Tao Source,*
> *Dear Divine,*

Dear all my spiritual fathers and mothers, angels, guides,
    and protectors,
I love you, honor you, and appreciate you.
Please give me a blessing to heal and transform my
    finances.
I am very grateful.
Thank you.

Breathing Power, Mind Power, Sound Power, and Tao Calligraphy Field Power

Use the Xi Qing Hu Zhuo (Inhale Positive, Exhale Negative) Breathing Power technique. Open the book to figure 7 (page 68) and breathe in the positive information, energy, and matter of the *Da Ai* Tao Calligraphy Field. As you inhale, visualize golden light from the *Da Ai* Tao Calligraphy Field coming to and gathering in your second energy chakra.

As you exhale, chant *Da Ai* and visualize the golden light radiating in all directions from your second energy chakra, filling your whole body as you exhale negative information, energy, and matter from your finances.

Continue to practice for at least ten minutes per time. You can practice several times per day. In fact, there is no time limit for this practice.

Zhong Mai Healing and Transformation

There is an ancient secret wisdom and practice to heal and transform the physical, emotional, mental, and spiritual bodies. In fact, this secret wisdom and practice can help heal and transform any aspect of life, including relationships and finances. It is named Zhong Mai Healing and Transformation. Zhong means *central*. Mai means *meridian*.

The Zhong Mai is a vertical channel in the center of the body from the bottom of the torso to the top of the head. It starts at the Hui Yin acupuncture point and ends at the Bai Hui acupuncture point. The Hui Yin acupuncture point is at the bottom of the torso. It lies between the anus and the external genitals on the perineum. The Bai Hui acupuncture point is at the center of the top of the head. Imagine a line running along the center of the top of your head, between the left and right sides. Now imagine a line connecting the tops of your ears running across the top of your head. The Bai Hui acupuncture point is at the intersection of these two lines.

These two acupuncture points (see figure 9) play a major role in balancing yin and yang. The Hui Yin point absorbs Mother Earth's energy. The Bai Hui point absorbs Heaven's energy. Mother Earth is yin. Heaven is yang. For five thousand years in traditional Chinese medicine, the number one principle for healing is to balance yin and yang.

Yang is the nature of fire. Fire is hot, ascending, and exciting. Yin is the nature of water. Water is cool, descending, and calm. Every system, every organ, every cell, and every part of the body are divided into yin and yang. For example, the back of the body is yang; the front of the body is yin. The upper part of the body is yang; the lower part is yin. The outside of the body is yang; the inside is yin.

The internal organs of the body are also categorized between yin and yang according to the Five Elements theory used in traditional Chinese medicine. The major yin-yang organ pairs are:

- Wood element: liver (yin)—gallbladder (yang)
- Fire element: heart (yin)—small intestine (yang)
- Earth element: spleen (yin)—stomach (yang)
- Metal element: lungs (yin)—large intestine (yang)
- Water element: kidneys (yin)—urinary bladder (yang)

In figure 8 on page 125, I share some additional basic wisdom of Five Elements theory for the physical body, emotional body, and more.[6]

The wisdom goes deeper. Every organ is divided into yin and yang. Every cell is also divided into yin and yang. Yin yang balance is healing. Excessive or insufficient yin causes sickness. Excessive or insufficient yang also causes sickness.

The Zhong Mai runs through and connects with seven major energy centers or chakras. In traditional Tao teaching, they are called gears:

---

[6] For deeper wisdom about Five Elements theory, see my book *Soul Healing Miracles: Ancient and New Sacred Wisdom, Knowledge, and Practical Techniques for Healing the Spiritual, Mental, Emotional, and Physical Bodies* (Dallas, Texas/Toronto, Ontario: BenBella Books/Heaven's Library Publication Corp.,2013).

Element	Yin Organ	Yang Organ	Sense	Body Tissue
Wood	Liver	Gallbladder	Eyes Sight	Tendons Nails
Fire	Heart	Small Intestine	Tongue Taste	Blood Vessels
Earth	Spleen	Stomach	Mouth Lips Speech	Muscles
Metal	Lungs	Large Intestine	Nose Smell	Skin
Water	Kidneys	Urinary Bladder	Ears Hearing	Bones Joints

Element	Unbalanced Emotion	Balanced Emotion	Body Fluid	Finger
Wood	Anger	Patience	Tears	Index
Fire	Depression Anxiety Excitability	Joy	Sweat	Middle
Earth	Worry	Love Compassion	Saliva	Thumb
Metal	Grief Sadness	Courage	Mucus	Ring
Water	Fear	Calmness	Urine	Little

Figure 8. Five Elements

1st energy chakra: 海地轮 Gear at the Bottom of the Ocean

2nd energy chakra: 水轮 Water Gear

3rd energy chakra: 日轮 Sun Gear

4th energy chakra: 火轮 Fire Gear

5th energy chakra: 风轮 Wind Gear

6th energy chakra: 月轮 Moon Gear

7th energy chakra: 天轮 Heaven Gear

These are the central spaces in the body. See figure 9.

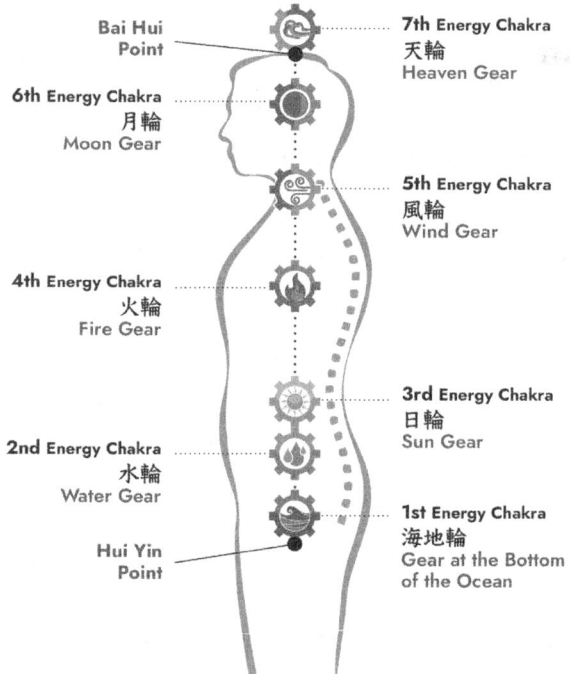

Figure 9. Seven Energy Chakras or Gears

The Zhong Mai also goes through San Jiao, which is often called the Triple Burner or Triple Warmer in English. It consists of three major spaces in the body. The Lower Jiao is the space in the torso below the level of the navel. The Middle Jiao is the space between the levels of the navel and the diaphragm. The Upper Jiao is the space above the diaphragm. See figure 10.

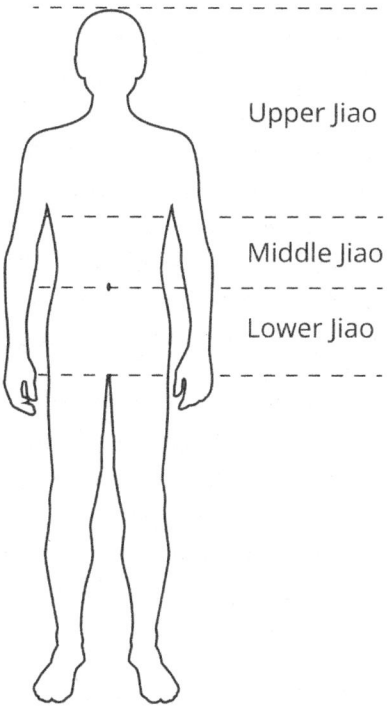

Figure 10. San Jiao

In traditional Chinese medicine, San Jiao is the pathway of qi and body fluids.

中脉一通, 百脉通

zhong mai yi tong, bai mai tong

If the central meridian flows freely, all meridians flow freely.

三焦畅通, 百病消除

san jiao chang tong, bai bing xiao chu

If San Jiao flows freely, all sicknesses are removed.

For the central meridian to flow freely, blockages in all seven energy chakras or gears must be removed. Blockages are negative shen qi jing. Each energy chakra connects closely with various aspects of our soul, heart, mind, and body. For example, the third energy chakra or Sun Gear connects with the Wood element, including the liver, gallbladder, eyes, tendons, and anger, and with the Water element, including the kidneys, urinary bladder, ears, bones, joints, and fear, while the sixth energy chakra or Moon Gear is very important for developing mind intelligence.

All seven energy chakras or gears together connect with every aspect of our soul, heart, mind, and body. Therefore, zhong mai yi tong, bai mai tong. This means *if the central meridian flows freely, all meridians flow freely.* It is vital to heal and transform the seven energy chakras and the Zhong Mai for all healing and transformation in our soul, heart, mind, and body.

San jiao chang tong, bai bing xiao chu (*if San Jiao flows freely, all sicknesses are removed*) tells us it is also vital to heal and transform negative shen qi jing in San Jiao for all healing and transformation.

What is the best way to heal and transform the seven energy chakras, the Zhong Mai, and San Jiao?

Is there a way to heal and transform the seven energy chakras, the Zhong Mai, and San Jiao together?

My answer is *yes*! I am honored to share this secret and sacred way in the next section.

Qi Channel

The Qi Channel is the most important energy channel in the body. The Qi Channel starts from the Hui Yin acupuncture point, goes up the Zhong Mai to the Bai Hui acupuncture point, then turns down through the back of the head and in front of the spinal column, through Wai Jiao, returning to the Hui Yin acupuncture point. See figure 11.

Wai Jiao is the biggest space in the body. It is the space in the back of the head and in front of the entire spinal column. See figure 11 on the next page. San Jiao and Wai Jiao partially overlap, so they are closely related. Specifically, San Jiao (Lower, Middle, and Upper) is like three rivers, and Wai Jiao is the ocean into which they flow. If San Jiao is blocked, Wai Jiao will be blocked. Therefore, if Wai Jiao is clear, San Jiao will be clear as well. Remember the ancient wisdom: san jiao chang tong, bai bing xiao chu (*if San Jiao flows freely, all sicknesses are removed*).

The Qi Channel connects the seven energy chakras or gears, the Zhong Mai, and Wai Jiao. Therefore, there is a way to heal and transform the seven energy chakras, the

Zhong Mai, and San Jiao together. What is the way? In one sentence:

To heal and transform the Qi Channel is to heal and transform the seven energy chakras, the Zhong Mai, San Jiao, and Wai Jiao together, which supports healing and transformation of the physical body, emotional body, mental body, spiritual body, relationships, finances, and every aspect of life.

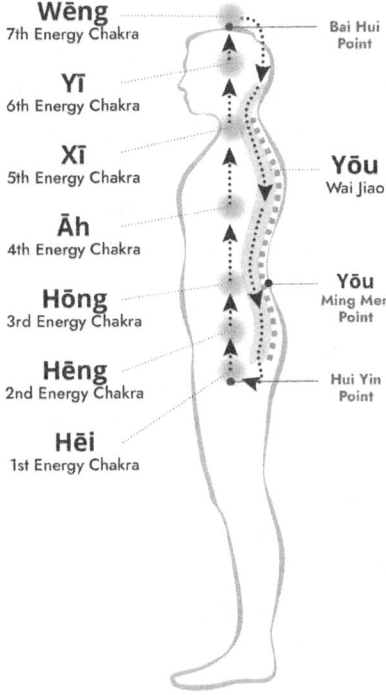

Wēng
7th Energy Chakra

Bai Hui
Point

Yī
6th Energy Chakra

Xī
5th Energy Chakra

Yōu
Wai Jiao

Āh
4th Energy Chakra

Hōng
3rd Energy Chakra

Yōu
Ming Men
Point

Hēng
2nd Energy Chakra

Hui Yin
Point

Hēi
1st Energy Chakra

Wai Jiao is the shaded space in the back of the head
and in front of the spinal column.

Figure 11. Qi Channel and Wai Jiao

What is the way to heal and transform the Qi Channel?

I received secret and sacred mantras from the Source for the seven energy chakras or gears and Wai Jiao. See figure 11.

- The secret mantra for the 1st energy chakra is Hei (pronounced *hay*).

- The secret mantra for the 2nd energy chakra is Heng (pronounced *hung*).

- The secret mantra for the 3rd energy chakra is Hong (pronounced *hōng*).

- The secret mantra for the 4th energy chakra is Ah (pronounced *ah*).

- The secret mantra for the 5th energy chakra is Xi (pronounced *shee*).

- The secret mantra for the 6th energy chakra is Yi (pronounced *ee*).

- The secret mantra for the 7th energy chakra is Weng (pronounced *wung*).

- The secret mantra for Wai Jiao is You (pronounced *yō*).

Therefore, the secret and sacred mantra for the Qi Channel is:

Hay, Hung, Hong, Ah, Shee, Ee Wung, yō

Hei Heng Hong Ah Xi Yi Weng You

For true healing and transformation of any part of the body, chant this mantra three times per day, ten minutes per time. I have created an animation where you can chant with me. You can also apply Mind Power to do the visualizations shown in the animation.

You can view the animation of the practice of the mantra for the Qi Channel through this QR code:

or on this webpage: **https://tchtda.heavenslibrary.com**

For best benefits, remember to apply Soul Power with the Say Hello Healing and Transformation technique, before you begin chanting:

"Say hello" to inner souls:

> *Dear my Qi Channel, seven energy chakras, Zhong Mai,*
>   *San Jiao, and Wai Jiao,*
> *I love you.*
> *You have the power to clear and boost yourselves.*
> *Do a great job.*
> *Thank you.*

"Say hello" to outer souls:

> *Dear the animation and secret, sacred mantra for the Qi*
>   *Channel,*
> *I love you, honor you, and appreciate you.*

Please clear and boost my Qi Channel and everything
   along its path.
I am very grateful.
Thank you.

Then, chant—with or without the animation—for ten minutes or more.

In fact, there is no time limit for doing the practice shown in the animation. For chronic pain and life-threatening conditions, do the practice for the Qi Channel for one to two hours a day. The benefits could be beyond your comprehension. I have applied this secret wisdom and practice to create many heart-touching and amazing results. I am delighted to release this as one of the highest self-healing secrets for humanity. My message of healing is:

I have the power to heal myself.
You have the power to heal yourself.
Together we have the power to heal the world.

To promote qi flow in the Zhong Mai is to heal the whole body.

To promote qi flow in San Jiao is to heal the whole body.

To promote qi flow in Wai Jiao is to heal the whole body.

To promote qi flow in the Qi Channel, one could get even faster and better results for healing the whole body.

When we are sick, we need doctors. We need healthcare professionals. I support all conventional and alternative and complementary medicines, all healing modalities. I just want you and humanity to realize that the human body has a self-restoring system. We need to activate it. We need to realize we can do amazing healing beyond our comprehension. I wish each reader to understand my message and to do more practice.

Practice. Practice. Practice.
Heal. Heal. Heal.
Transform. Transform. Transform.
Restore your health as quickly as possible.

Heal and Transform Depression and Anxiety with the Tao Calligraphy Tao Zhuan You Yu Jiao Lü Field

YOU COULD RECEIVE benefits from Tao Calligraphy Transformative Art that are beyond comprehension. Tao Calligraphy Transformative Art can help you heal, prevent sickness, and transform your health, relationships, finances, spiritual journey, and every aspect of life.

In this chapter, I focus on healing and transforming depression and anxiety. More and more people are suffering from depression or anxiety. It is estimated that about 1 in 13 adults in America suffer from major depressive disorder. Anxiety and depression also affect many children, from teenagers to very young children, and have generally increased over the last two decades. The societal effects of the coronavirus pandemic have accelerated the rate of increase since 2020. One meta-analysis completed in August 2021 concluded that rates of depression and anxiety in children worldwide may have doubled since the start of the coronavirus pandemic. For American adolescents, depression and suicide are unquestionably major concerns. More than one-third of them have persistent feelings of sadness or hopelessness. About 1 in 5 seriously considered attempting suicide, and about 1 in 10 actually attempted suicide.

For this book, I have created a transformative art tool: the Tao Calligraphy *Tao Zhuan You Yu Jiao Lü* 道转忧郁焦虑. Tao is the Source. Zhuan means *to transform*. You yu means *depression*. Jiao lü means *anxiety*. The *Tao Zhuan You Yu Jiao Lü* Tao Calligraphy Field covers the entire heart area.

Ancient wisdom teaches that the heart houses the mind and soul. Depression and anxiety are shen qi jing blockages in the heart area. (See also figure 8 on page 125.) To transform depression and anxiety, we need to clear these shen qi jing blockages in the heart area.

The *Tao Zhuan You Yu Jiao Lü* Tao Calligraphy carries Source love, light, frequency, and vibration and most-positive information, energy, and matter, which could transform the negative information, energy, and matter of depression and anxiety in the heart area. This Tao Calligraphy is for your use on the front and back covers.

Da Dao zhi jian 大道至简 means *the greatest Tao is extremely simple*. Applying this Tao Calligraphy to transform depression and anxiety is extremely simple.

Another ancient statement I often share is:

> *If you want to know if a pear is sweet, taste it.*

To this, I add:

*If you want to know if Tao Calligraphy healing works,
experience it.*

Follow the techniques I explain below. Remember to practice more and more. Quantity leads quality. If you feel better sooner, congratulations. Continue to practice until you are healed. If you do not feel better right away, be patient. Not every case will respond immediately. Practice persistently. The negative information, energy, and matter of your depression or anxiety are transforming. Tangible results will follow.

In chapter eleven, I share heart-touching stories of healing and transformation of depression and anxiety through the Tao Calligraphy Field. In chapter twelve, Dr. Peter Hudoba discusses clinical research on Tao Calligraphy for depression and anxiety.

Let's practice receiving healing, prevention, and transformation from the *Tao Zhuan You Yu Jiao Lü* Tao Calligraphy Field.

We will use the Xi Qing Hu Zhuo Breathing Power technique that I introduced in chapter eight. This is the key practice technique for healing all sickness. This technique will be used in all books in my Tao Calligraphy series.

Xi Qing Hu Zhuo (Inhale Positive, Exhale Negative) Practice for Depression and Anxiety

Apply the Six Power Techniques.

Body Power

Put the Tao Calligraphy *Tao Zhuan You Yu Jiao Lü* (on the front or back cover) over your heart.

Soul Power

"Say hello" to inner souls:

> *Dear soul, heart, mind, and body* (or *shen qi jing*) *of my heart,*
> *I love you, honor you, and appreciate you.*
> *You have the power to heal and transform yourself.*
> *Do a great job.*
> *Thank you.*

"Say hello" to outer souls:

> *Dear the Tao Calligraphy* Tao Zhuan You Yu Jiao Lü *Field,*
> *Dear Tao Source,*
> *Dear Divine,*
> *Dear all my spiritual fathers and mothers, angels, guides, and protectors,*
> *I love you, honor you, and appreciate you.*
> *Please give me a healing to transform my depression and anxiety.*
> *I am very grateful.*
> *Thank you.*

Breathing Power, Mind Power, Sound Power, and Tao Calligraphy Field Power

Inhale and visualize golden light from the *Tao Zhuan You Yu Jiao Lü* Tao Calligraphy Field gathering in and around your heart.

As you exhale, chant *Tao Calligraphy heals my depression and anxiety.* At the same time, visualize the golden light radiating out in all directions from the heart area to remove negative information, energy, and matter of depression and anxiety.

You can view the animation of the practice with the *Tao Zhuan You Yu Jiao Lü* Tao Calligraphy through this QR code:

or on this webpage: **https://tchtda.heavenslibrary.com**

Continue the breathing in, breathing out practice. It is best to practice for at least ten minutes per time, and you can practice several times per day. In fact, there is no time limit for this practice. For chronic or severe depression and anxiety, practice several times a day so that your total practice time each day is one to two hours. The benefits could be beyond your comprehension.

I wrote the *Tao Zhuan You Yu Jiao Lü* Tao Calligraphy on the front and back covers in June 2022 during a healing session webcast to hundreds of people around the world. I am delighted to share some of the many reports of the participants' experiences as and after we practiced together in the Tao Calligraphy *Tao Zhuan You Yu Jiao Lü* Field. Many people experienced the Tao Calligraphy Field even as I was writing this Tao Calligraphy.

I sincerely wish you to use the Tao Calligraphy *Tao Zhuan You Yu Jiao Lü* Field more for healing, prevention, and transformation of your depression and anxiety.

Many people worldwide have already experienced a profound transformation of their depression and anxiety from the Tao Calligraphy *Tao Zhuan You Yu Jiao Lü* Transformative Art Field. Enjoy some of their stories in the next chapter. May you be inspired to use the Tao Calligraphy Field more. The Tao Calligraphy Transformative Art Field is available for you here and now.

Heart-touching Stories of Tao Calligraphy Field Transformation of Depression and Anxiety

I AM DELIGHTED to share some of the stories of healing and transformation of depression or anxiety that participants in my online events have recently reported. All of these reports are related to applying the Transformative Art Field of the Tao Calligraphy *Tao Zhuan You Yu Jiao Lü* that I wrote in June 2022. All of these reports were received within one week of my creating this Tao Calligraphy, which I am now releasing to humanity on the front and back covers of this book. We in fact received many more heart-touching stories—far too many to include all of them in a brief chapter. What you can read here is a representative sampling.

May you be moved, touched, and inspired by these stories.

May you know that there is hope—for you, your loved ones, your friends, your colleagues—for anyone who suffers from depression or anxiety.

The Tao Calligraphy Field brings this hope.

The Tao Calligraphy Field is here for you and for humanity now.

Enjoy these stories of hope fulfilled.

ॐ ॐ ॐ

Twenty years of heaviness transform to inner peace and happiness

Twenty years ago, a friend asked me if I could feel joy. This question made me realize that something really big was missing in my life: happiness.

I am an occupational therapist and naturopath. I had a comfortable normal life with a family and a good job, but I was not satisfied. Heaviness was always with me. There were only a few moments when I could really feel joy. I did not realize that I had depression because it was so normal for me.

A few days ago, I had the opportunity to be in the Tao Calligraphy Field for healing depression and anxiety. During the meditation with the Tao Calligraphy for Transforming Depression and Anxiety, my mind and heart became calm. My heart is so often nervous. In fact, I was constantly anxious and nervous for thirty years. During the meditation with this Tao Calligraphy, a feeling of inner peace and happiness arose. It was like all the clouds of heaviness were removed and the sky was blue again. I started to smile and there were no worries in my mind anymore.

Such a relief. I am so grateful to Master Sha and the huge healing power of the Tao Calligraphy Field.

— S. S.

Depressed and sad since childhood but heart now at peace

I have lived with depression and sadness since childhood, so I know how hard it is to transform this pain when it is deeply anchored in the consciousness and the body.

In a recent event, Master Sha created a Tao Calligraphy for healing depression and anxiety. When we practiced with the new calligraphy, I had a hard time staying connected, but I did my best to really go deeper into absorbing the light. I did not feel much difference immediately after the session. But the day after, everything has changed. My whole chest area is more open and my heart is at peace. I had a wonderful dream about new possibilities.

I fully realized the power within this incredible Tao Calligraphy when I was hurt again at work by a co-worker. Not long ago, this would have knocked me down emotionally and mentally for days. This time I went through the experience with ease. I am astonished not to have the usual feeling of depression—and there is no sadness either! That is a miracle, and I am deeply grateful that such a tool will become available for everyone through Master Sha's book.

For me, Tao Calligraphy is the quickest and most efficient instrument we can have to transform suffering.

— D. F.

All unpleasant emotions dissolved

I am a TCM practitioner, acupuncturist, and expert diagnostician. I live in a beautiful northern Oregon coastal city in the United States. I am passionate about helping people to become healthier with natural and holistic medicine and soul, mind, and body medicine techniques, and I have served thousands of clients.

At times, I have felt that I've experienced vicarious emotions and trauma that my clients have gone through and shared with me. Over the past few weeks, I have had some feelings of anxiety and depression due to hearing about unpleasant things that have occurred in their lives. It was serendipitous that I received an invitation to listen to Master Sha and receive this special blessing for anxiety and depression from his new Tao Calligraphy.

I have experienced amazing healing effects from Master Sha's techniques in the past. However, this most recent blessing was a new experience! When the blessing began, I felt tingling waves of energy reverberating throughout my body, followed by a calm and relaxing feeling in my chest, stillness in my mind, and peace in my heart. I feel like I am a different person right now! All of the unpleasant emotions dissolved so quickly. It is truly a miracle that this is available to us. I truly wish everyone could experience how amazing this healing is.

— J. C.

Feeling uplifted, lighter, and brighter

I am a data scientist with 10+ years of experience doing analytics.

After reaching the deepest point of depression in my life, I began a healing journey. Tao Healing Hands and the Tao wisdom shared by Dr. and Master Sha have been a sustainable practice to stay happy and healthy. For the last couple of days, though, I had been struggling with personal and professional issues and energies that were bothering me. By joining his event, New Pearls of Wisdom, I was able to ground and feel uplifted and happier, and the depression, lower vibrational feelings, monkey mind, and energy pulling me back like a heavy weight on my shoulders were immediately transformed.

I cannot find enough words to express my gratitude for the Tao Calligraphy for transforming depression and anxiety, Master Sha, and all his team. By the end of the event, I had already received a call for a new job and ideas for a personal project that I am working on. Immediately, I could feel my energy was lighter and brighter. I am so grateful.

— D. M.

Have been waiting for this for thirty years

In 1992, at the age of twenty-seven, I overdosed on sleeping pills. I had lost control and just watched myself doing it and couldn't intervene. I was brought to intensive care and then to a closed psychiatric unit for a week. I felt like I was in the wrong movie, with no control over my life. My brain was like a TV where someone switched the channel every few seconds.

In the twenty years that followed, I spent lots of time with trauma therapists, which was helpful for understanding what was going on, but it didn't heal my condition. Between 1995 and 2006, I was admitted to psychiatric hospitals at least ten times, sometimes for more than two months at a time. I learned that I could go there on my own whenever I felt that the inner pressure was so strong that I was close to losing control again and might try to commit suicide.

I met Master Sha in 2013, just when I was about to move from Germany to Austria to live with my partner. During the next nine years, I was blessed to receive high-frequency light transmissions, which are always with me. I completed several educational programs with Tao Academy and received empowerments to heal myself and others. I worked very hard helping others to heal and transform their lives. In late 2019, I had a total burnout. I finally took responsibility for my life again and pulled the emergency brake before I might lose control.

I stepped back from my volunteer assignments and told my partner that I couldn't do anything for a while. I gained a lot of weight. At times, I had difficulty even taking a shower. Cooking lunch was another huge challenge; most of the time we ordered food from restaurants. In early 2022, I realized that I had severe depression again. This was a huge relief. My condition had a name, and I could stop beating myself up for all the things I wanted to do but just could not do. I started to ask for blessings for depression and I also received spiritual light transmissions for depression. My digestive system had become quite disordered, so this was my second issue. Finally, I felt I was on the right track and the chanting and transmissions did something. But still, it felt like a drop in a bucket.

Last night in the New Pearls of Wisdom workshop with Master Sha, he wrote a calligraphy to heal and transform depression and *anxiety. A glimpse of hope emerged as I sat down to join the practice. At first, I felt a wave of warm light entering my heart area. Then my whole body became very hot. My chest widened and I could breathe much deeper. My digestive system calmed down. This was one of the most impressive blessings I have ever received. And it even lasted after waking up this morning! I feel that this is what I have been waiting for all these years, and it is huge.*

I am totally thrilled that Master Sha's new book will be about healing depression and will include this Tao Calligraphy. I can't wait to get the book. I am deeply grateful. Thank you, Master Sha.

— E. K.

Very strong healing effect—almost immediately!

I have struggled intensely with "long Covid" for over two years. Although I have made monumental strides in my recovery, a persistent issue is anxiety caused by the damage done to my nervous system by the virus. Over the past two years, I have seen a trauma specialist and received two types of treatments, and also used very advanced light and sound therapy, as well as regular acupuncture and herbal therapy, special breathing, and cold therapy.

Today, during Master Sha's New Pearls of Wisdom healing demonstration event, my nervous system became so relaxed I had a hard time even staying conscious. There was a consistent, heavy, warm, palpable energy flowing into the palms of my hands and penetrating straight into my heart. My whole energy field became intensely still, and it continued beyond the time of the actual healing blessing.

For someone like me, who has had severe pain and anxiety for so long and has tried so many things to heal, I know without question when something is effective or not. This Tao Calligraphy blessing produced a very strong healing effect in a very short time. Totally mind-blowing. Great achievement, Master Sha! Genius healing.

— K. D.

A priceless experience

I was feeling some deep-rooted pain inside my heart. The pain was at about a level 4 to 5 on a scale of 0 to 10. In stressful situations, I could feel this area more. It would affect how I reacted to challenging situations. During Master Sha's session with the new Tao Calligraphy for healing depression and anxiety, I felt a lot of expansion in my heart area, and gradually all the painful blockages disappeared in such a short time. I felt no pain inside my heart. Absolutely incredible!

After a few hours of being in the event in the high-frequency field, I felt more inner happiness, peace, and trust that whatever comes, I can trust in the process. A priceless experience. Thank you so much, Master Sha and the Tao Calligraphy Field.

— A. S.

I can breathe and function

I am thirty-seven years old. Certain circumstances I faced in my childhood planted the seeds of depression and other negative emotions such as anger within me. I was a quiet child who internalized everything. Little did I know that when I would reach the ages of 13–14, I would start to exhibit signs of depression, anger, anxiety, and more.

As the years went by, I would go into regular bouts of depression and anxiety, yet I never told anyone. I would suffer in silence. I started to develop chronic stress/anxiety and depression. It would happen so often that I started to get palpitations in my heart every day. I had little or no self-love, self-confidence, or self-esteem. To the world, it looked as though I was leading a good life where everything was provided by my family. I do have a lovely family, yet I always felt lonely, anxious, and depressed. After I got to know Master Sha in late 2019 and truly started to understand Master Sha's wisdom, teachings, and boundless love for everyone, I started to transform little-by-little.

In today's session, when Master Sha taught us to practice with the Tao Calligraphy for healing depression and anxiety and blessed us with it, I felt so many layers of deep blockages lift, and peace prevailed throughout my being. I feel like this peaceful emptiness has permeated throughout my entire self. I feel a deeper stillness within me, and my body feels completely relaxed. I feel a lot of the internal noise in my being has just left me! Each and every part of my body feels so deeply relaxed, as if every cell and the spaces between the cells released years of so much pressure, and I can breathe and function more freely.

I am so grateful to have been in this field because I feel that so much got released in a few precious minutes of practice! This is a truly priceless gift for those of us who have to face the challenges of depression and anxiety regularly. Master Sha, you truly understand what each of us goes through individually and collectively, and you do everything you can to help alleviate our suffering.

— H. S.

From severe anxiety to deep contentment

Two-and-a-half years ago, I had an emergency surgery and awoke paralyzed from the navel down and in excruciating pain. Everything changed in this one moment: relationships (people I was friends with for over twenty years didn't call anymore), work (I was unable to continue work as a nurse or in any other capacity), health in all aspects, finances (huge impact as I was now dependent upon social services), emotions, and more. I had to experience various medical diagnoses and treatments, with varying experiences with doctors and nurses.

Severe anxiety and depressive moods developed. At times, they were so severe that I didn't want to leave my apartment. During today's event, Master Sha created a beautiful new Tao Calligraphy to heal depression and anxiety and we practiced with it. After about fifteen minutes of practice, I suddenly could feel a deep calm and sense of contentment washing over me. I felt free and light. It was such a relief! I could have stayed in this condition for the rest of my life.

I am so excited about Master Sha's next book with this Tao Calligraphy! Thank you, Master Sha, for offering this opportunity to release so much!

— N. K.

Anxiety and fear washed away as my entire being is transformed

I have suffered from bipolar depression for about six years. I have been hospitalized for this illness several times and have been on medication for several years. This condition causes me to feel very unbalanced and unstable mentally and emotionally. After receiving blessings from the Tao Calligraphy for Transforming Depression and Anxiety during an online event with Master Sha, I felt so much more balance and joy. I felt as if the anxiety and fear had washed away.

The Tao Calligraphy Master Sha wrote, Tao Zhuan You Yu Jiao Lü, *was so powerful! Not only did it transform the bipolar depression, but I also felt my digestion ease and my whole body's health transform! I also requested healing for restless legs, which I believe are triggered by stress. After receiving the blessing, my legs felt grounded and nourished. I know this beautiful calligraphy and event with Master Sha transformed my entire being.*

— B. O.

A thousand thank you's

Yesterday I joined the New Pearls of Wisdom with Master Sha for healing for my anxiety and depression. I have had suicidal thoughts due to negative thoughts and issues that have affected my life. I was also depressed. At times, I thought I did not want to go on. It started with Covid-19 and things got worse. I have been suffering with a strange condition for some time that involves my breathing, circulation, and metabolism. I believe it could be linked to my anxiety. I also have some menopausal symptoms that have added to my brain not feeling very calm.

I have also noticed that my breathing is very shallow at night and my body swells. I have had "pins and needles" in my hands and feet and sometimes really bad numbness. I did the healing practices yesterday with the Tao Calligraphy for transforming depression and anxiety and, for the first time in months, I did not have breathing problems, tightness in my chest, numbness and tingling in my hands, or swelling in my body. This is a miracle from God in the Tao Calligraphy Healing Field of light brought down by Master Sha for us all. I also got Covid-19 again this week and it has also helped with those symptoms This is the second time that Dr. Sha's healing wisdom has helped me in my life. He also cured my eye condition and an operation was avoided.

A thousand thank you's to you, Dr. Sha, and your team. I will continue to spread your work to others so they know and benefit from your healing love for humanity.

— P. E.

Life is worth living again

I am a Sound Healing Practitioner and Teacher and also work as a support worker for complex care clients. I have two daughters and two grandsons. I have lived in the U.K. since 2000 with

*my second husband, my feline tribe, and my horse. I have suf-
fered from depression and anxiety since I was eighteen. That was
when I felt for the first time the sensation of falling into a deep,
dark hole of despair, and this deep yearning that there must be
more to life than just growing up, working, drinking, and then
dying. This felt like the dark night of the soul, and my inner
search to find answers to what was missing began. It felt like so
much darkness was around me, and something heavy and
gloomy was clouding my being. Something was missing and I
felt weight pressing down on me.*

*After the birth of my second daughter, I suffered from severe
panic attacks that would awaken me in the middle of the night
with my heart racing. I would have the feeling that all was lost
and I was doomed. Apart from when I was a kid and loved life,
I seemed to often awaken with the feeling that life was a heavy
burden and that I would not have the strength to deal with it.
My mother suffered from anxiety when she was young too. After
the divorce from my first husband, I had suicidal thoughts that
continued when I moved to the U.K. to be with my second husband. I never went to the doctor and I suffered in silence. This
is the first time that I am talking openly about what I have been
through. I have found my own little ways to cope and deal with
the panic and depression. But there is still this gray filter that
seems to damp everything down, especially the last few months.
It has been worse again, which led to a disruption in my sleep
pattern.*

*There is inability to focus and concentrate, relax, and no moti-
vation to do things. I have felt very overwhelmed by life and have
had problems waking up in the morning and facing the day. My
sense of smell and taste were compromised, and I was unable to*

relax or quiet my mind. My energy was very low and I felt very tired, which made me very irritable. It felt like I was a rubber band that was overstretched. My heart felt heavy and numb. I would fill the lack of joy and happiness by eating vast amounts of chocolate and other sweet stuff, as I could not feel the sweetness of life.

On June 21, 2022, I knew that this special event with Master Sha was happening, but I could not find the link to join the online event and I felt very depressed as I knew that it was very important for me to attend. I felt I was at my lowest point and very tired of life. I went to bed early and awoke early. And the experience that I had that morning of June 22 I can only describe as the following. As Master Sha wrote the Tao Calligraphy for Transforming Depression and Anxiety, he brought the energy field of healing and transforming anxiety and depression to Mother Earth. Master Sha had channeled down this energy into the Earth Field. So, when I sat that morning and offered myself a Tao Healing Hands Blessing and connected to Tao, this energy came in and flooded my whole system. It touched my heart so deeply and caused all the pain that I had pushed down to come up. All of the suffering surfaced and came out in tears and a huge release happened. Waves of tears and the deepest pain surfaced. I felt so much love from the spirit world wrap around me. After releasing all of this pain, my heart became peaceful and quiet. I felt like a huge burden had lifted and my insides had been washed and cleansed.

I was so grateful and felt so much love in my heart for Master Sha and the Tao. Shortly after, I found the link for the "New Pearls of Wisdom" event with Master Sha and watched it with a deeply grateful heart. I was healed by the information that was brought down by Master Sha in the form of this beautiful calligraphy. Now three days later, I feel such a huge shift in my life. I can feel the sweetness of life again, my sense of smell is elevated, and I can taste again. Everything seems more vibrant and alive. I feel the greatest joy in my heart and I am so grateful for this new Tao Calligraphy and this new book by Master Sha.

I feel the gray filter has been taken away and life is colorful again and worth living. A huge burden has been lifted, and I can breathe deeper and easier again. Thank you so, so much, Master Sha, for your service. Thank you, Tao, for healing me.

— C. M.

The impossible became possible

Before discovering Master Sha's wisdom and the Tao Calligraphy Healing Field, I suffered with deep anxiety and depression. Even though I have always been known as a very bubbly and joyful person, I went through a huge life transition in my mid-twenties. I had been dealing with heartbreak after the end of an eight-year relationship with the love of my life, and after ten years of working in the film and television industry, I hit burnout.

I took a year off work to travel and volunteer in India, and this experience led me into a huge spiritual awakening. But I continued to spiral into deep anxiety around the purpose of my life and what I was meant to do on this planet. During this time, I was drowning in school debt and credit card debt with extremely high interest rates. I couldn't see a way out. I also had physical health challenges and suffered an injury to my hand which left my right thumb unable to bend permanently and simultaneously was suffering from severe cystic acne. I felt hopeless and awoke every day feeling like I was drowning. I questioned my existence and wondered how I would ever make it through.

Then I discovered the Tao Calligraphy Healing Field. I began attending weekly sessions. I found myself tracing Tao Calligraphy at home and connecting to the field, chanting Tao healing mantras, and doing forgiveness practice. Over a few weeks, I began to feel significant improvement. Over the following months, my condition totally improved. My emotions stabilized. My outlook on life got so much brighter.

Now years later, I can confirm that my life has progressively improved, beyond what I could have ever imagined. It is truly a miracle. My anxiety and depression completely resolved and have not returned. I feel excited and grateful every single morning when I wake up. My heart has expanded and my consciousness feels lighter. I discovered a way that I could heal myself using the Tao Calligraphy Healing Field. I've experienced feeling like life was a dark tunnel, with no way out. I've experienced feeling like I was drowning without the ability to come up for air. I've experienced what it feels like to question if life is worth living every day. And because of the Tao Calligraphy Healing Field, I've experienced the seemingly impossible become possible.

I have discovered that there IS light at the end of the tunnel. I've experienced that it IS possible to not only come up for air, but stay there. I now experience what it's like to wake up every day and know my life has purpose and to live my purpose. I am eternally grateful.

— A. C.

My heart feels so peaceful and calm

Growing up a child of immigrant parents who had high expectations of their children—expectations that I could not meet—made me very anxious. As a result, I had no self-esteem and felt like a failure compared to my brother and sister who could do no wrong in my parents' eyes.

I was very quiet and hated talking in public. When I did speak, I spoke fast, believing what I had to say was unimportant. I remember instances when as a child I would have to go shopping with my mother. Because she did not speak English, I had to go to the counter to ask for items. I would shake with anxiety and my voice would be so quiet when I spoke that often the counterperson could not hear me and I had to repeat myself, which only made me feel worse.

My anxiety got worse as I grew older. In my teenage years, I started pulling out my hair, leaving bald patches, and scratching myself so hard that I bled. I had no control over things around me, but in my mind, pulling out my hair and scratching myself were oddly soothing as I felt I was in control of one thing in my life. For me, anxiety goes hand in hand with a negative mindset. I felt worthless and did not believe I deserved a good life. This became a self-fulfilling prophecy as I suffered from bad relationships, bad finances, bad health, and bad jobs as an adult.

I became a student of Master Sha in 2015 and, through his teachings and practices, I have been able to transform a lot of the negativity in my life to positivity, for which I am very grateful! However, all that is happening in the world today—war, high inflation, rising interest rates, supply chain issues, talk of reces-sion, and more—has made me very anxious. What if I lose my job? What if I can't pay my mortgage? What will happen to me?

Today's practice session with the transform depression and anx-iety Tao Calligraphy was a godsend. Before the session started, I was feeling quite anxious. On a scale of 1 to 10 with 10 being the most anxious, I was at level 7. The Tao Calligraphy Healing Field is so powerful! As we started breathing in the pure light and energy of the field and breathing out the negativity and tox-ins in our bodies, I could feel my heart vibrating. After practic-ing for twenty minutes with the Tao Calligraphy and Master Sha, my heart felt so peaceful and calm. I also received a message to not worry about the future, focus on the present, and that things will be alright! Thank you, Tao Calligraphy. Thank you, Master Sha!

— Y. L.

ॐ ॐ ॐ

I thank each of you who shared your story, including the many more of you whose stories are not included in this book. I am delighted that you have received great benefits from the Tao Calligraphy Transformative Art Field. I thank you for your gratitude and appreciation.

I also offer my greatest gratitude to Tao Source, to the Tao Calligraphy Transformative Art Field, and to all who have empowered me to be your servant. I am honored to serve you. I am honored to serve humanity with Tao Calligraphy Transformative Art.

I love my heart and soul
I love all humanity
Join hearts and souls together
Love, peace, and harmony
Love, peace, and harmony

Scientific Research on Tao Calligraphy Field Transformation of Depression by Peter Hudoba, M.D.

I AM A FORMER neurosurgeon, currently practicing non-surgical spinal care. I received my medical degree from the University of Komenskeho, Czechoslovakia. After relocating to Canada, I was involved in pioneering research in Neurosciences at McMaster University. I then went on to study neurosurgery at the University of Toronto before joining Royal University Hospital in Saskatchewan as a full staff neurosurgeon consultant. During this time, I also taught at the University of Saskatchewan as an Assistant Professor and served as Head of Neurosurgical postgraduate programs there from 1999 to 2000.

Over the years I have received several awards, including Excellence in Teaching Award from the University of Saskatchewan and Thomas P. Morley Neurosurgical Resident prize from the University of Toronto. I have presented at many scientific conferences in Canada, the United States, United Kingdom, and elsewhere.

I retired as a neurosurgeon in 2001 to devote more time to research on alternative healing methods. I currently have a private practice offering non-operative spinal care in Vancouver, British Columbia. For the last nineteen years, I have worked with Sha Research Foundation, initially as CEO and President, and currently as Director of Research. At the same time, I have also been very active with community and volunteer activities and travel to many countries to teach health-improving techniques.

For the last several years, Sha Research Foundation has formed research teams to study the effects of practices in Master Sha's Tao Calligraphy Transformative Art Field by subjects with depression. One study was done in Europe and two others in North America. In 2022, we also initiated a new study of the effects of Tao Calligraphy Field practices combined with the use of Tao Water. Of these four studies, two have successfully concluded, while the other two are still in progress as of this writing.

All Sha Research Foundation studies use conventional research study designs and well-recognized standardized research questionnaires to document changes in research subjects. For the past several years, we have studied the effects of Tao Calligraphy Transformative Art. To document individual cases, we use the NCI Best Case Series Program model. Our research studies are approved and monitored by IRB (institutional review board), except in Europe, where an ethics committee was the approver.

ॐ ௐ ౧౩

I am delighted to share general results and some individual cases from the recent European study.

Unipolar depression study
Hannover, Germany
Dr. Katharina Balonwu

I am a clinical psychologist and psychotherapist dealing with mental and psychiatric illnesses and emotional diseases. I train my patients in customized sessions to restore their health by changing dysfunctional thoughts, emotions, behaviors, actions, and activities. I had the honor to develop and design a research study and would like to introduce the results to you.

Comparative psychometric studies and questionnaires on the effects of Tao Calligraphy tracing meditation in patients with unipolar depression after twenty-five hours and fifty hours (Germany, 2020)

The World Health Organization (WHO) predicts unipolar depression will be the disease with the highest burden in industrialized nations by 2030. The risk of developing clinical depression during a lifetime is estimated to be between sixteen percent and twenty percent in Germany and internationally.

The research study was approved by the ethics committee of the Hamburg Chamber of Psychotherapists. This study involved twenty-three subjects (aged 21 to 63) suffering from unipolar depression. None of the subjects had any prior knowledge of Dr. and Master Zhi Gang Sha or his healing methods.

Subjects completed the standardized international psychometric questionnaires BDI–II, PHQ–9, HAM–D, and HAM–A at the beginning of the study, and after twenty-five hours and fifty hours of Tao Calligraphy tracing meditation with mantra chanting. Statistical analysis was done by the independent government-approved German Institute for Clinical Statistics in order to avoid bias and conflicts of interest.

Preliminary Group 1 results of the study were presented at the annual conference of the European Congress for Integrative Medicine in London, United Kingdom in November 2021 and published in 2022.

ANOVA analysis showed that all indexes exhibited statistically significant positive improvement.

Group 1 consisted of twenty-three subjects aged between 21 and 63 years, who had suffered from depression for one to forty-two years. Fifteen of the subjects were on antidepressive medication. Eleven had received inpatient treatment. All twenty-three study participants had received psychotherapeutic sessions.

The Beck Depression Inventory II (BDI–II) is a widely used self-reporting questionnaire to measure the presence and severity of depressive symptoms using twenty-one multiple-choice questions. Higher total scores indicate more severe depressive symptoms.

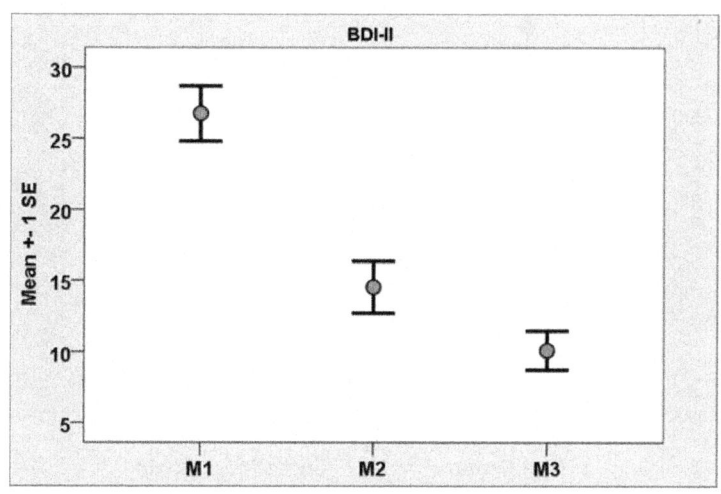

BDI-II Group 1, n=23, Changes M1, M2, M3

- After twenty-five hours of the meditation and chanting practice, the BDI–II score dropped from 26.74 to 14.52 (p<0.001).
- After fifty hours, the BDI–II score reduced further to 10.09 (p<0.001).
- This corresponds to an improvement of 59%.

The Patient Health Questionnaire–9 (PHQ–9) is a nine-question symptom assessment tool, scaling each of the nine DSM–V and ICD–10 depression criteria.

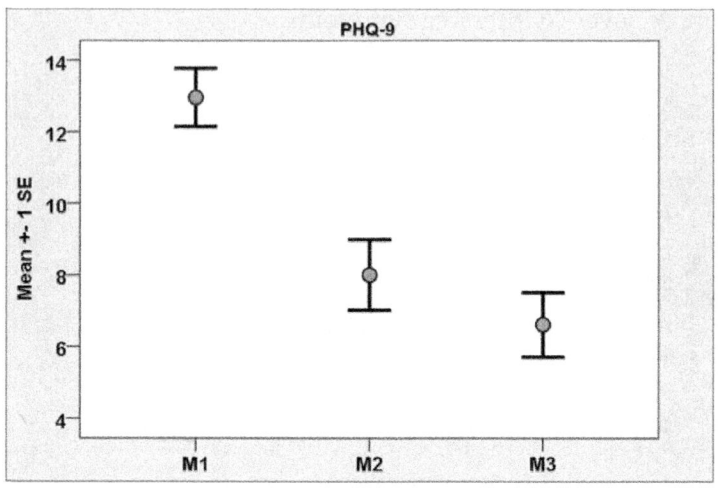

PHQ-9 Group 1, n=23, Changes M1, M2, M3

- The PHQ–9 score changed from 12.96 points to 8 (p<0.001) after twenty-five hours of the meditation and chanting practice.
- After fifty hours, the PHQ–9 score reduced further to 6.61 (p<0.001).
- This corresponds to an improvement of 44%.

The Hamilton Depression Rating Scale (HAM–D 21) is the most widely used clinician-administered depression assessment scale using twenty-one items with different scores. It was originally developed for hospital inpatients.

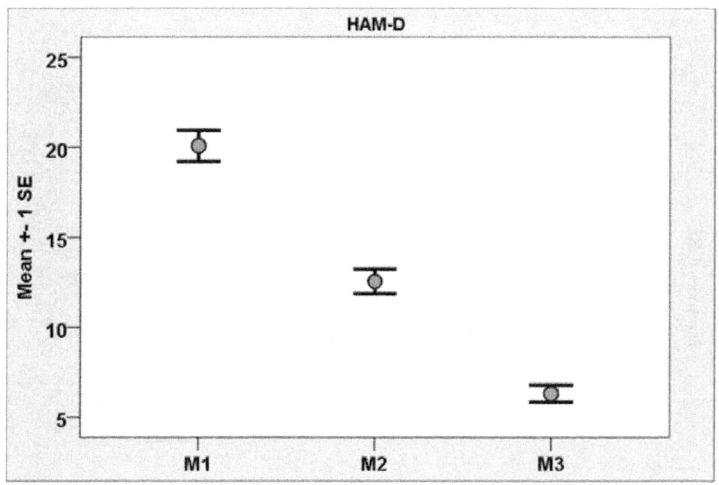

HAM-D Group 1, n=23, Changes M1, M2, M3

- After twenty-five hours of the meditation and chanting practice, the HAM–D score dropped from 20.09 points to 12.57 (p<0.001).
- After fifty hours, the HAM–D score reduced further to 6.35 (p<0.001).
- This corresponds to an improvement of 68%.

The Hamilton Anxiety Scale (HAM–A) was developed to measure the severity of anxiety symptoms. It is widely validated and still widely used in both clinical and research settings. The scale consists of fourteen items measuring both psychic and somatic anxiety.

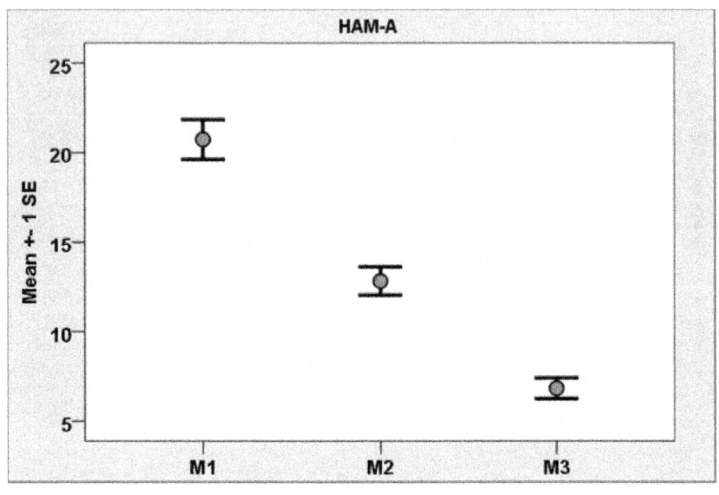

HAM-A Group 1, n=23, Changes M1, M2, M3

- The HAM–A score dropped from 20.74 to 12.83 (p<0.001) after twenty-five hours of meditation and chanting practice.
- After fifty hours, the HAM–A score reduced further to 6.8 (p<0.001).
- This corresponds to an improvement of 68%.

Group 1 results indicate that Tao Calligraphy tracing meditation combined with mantra chanting improved symptoms of unipolar depression markedly after twenty-five and fifty hours.

With the increase in depression and anxiety during the current coronavirus pandemic and in light of the World Health Organization's prognosis on unipolar depression, Tao Calligraphy tracing meditation has proven to be an important tool that significantly benefited the subject patients with unipolar depression.

I am honored to share details about two study subjects in this European study, followed by some individual cases from our North American studies.

Case Study A (European study)

A 45-year-old male participant with severe unipolar depression and anxiety symptoms was unable to trace due to strong tremors in both hands. He had the idea to stand and do Tao Calligraphy tai chi (body movement tracing) with open hands. He had suffered from unipolar depression since adolescence and had subsisted on social government funding for more than twenty years. He had been treated several times in psychiatric hospitals. Midway through the study, he started to work. He is now working part-time and free of all depression symptoms, emotionally stable, and happy. He has started a social life again after fifteen years.

Case Study B (European study)

This 23-year-old female flight attendant was very sad, depressed, and felt hopeless, because she had lost trust in life and love due to physical trauma. Her heart was very closed when she started the Tao Calligraphy tracing meditation. After twenty-five hours, she started to reconnect with her heart and emotions. Upon completing fifty hours of practice, she felt self-love again. She has fallen in love and is very happy. She has no longer has any depressive symptoms. She has even started attending a university.

ॐ ॐ ॐ

Here are some Success Cases from our North American research studies.

Case Study C (three-year follow-up study)

This 52-year-old female, a very successful performer at her work, suffered from a disconnection due to childhood trauma. She has experienced extreme stomach pains (level 9–10 on a scale of 0 to 10) after her mother nearly died when she was a child aged 5. Ever since, she has felt anxious and disconnected. Her symptoms became worse when she was 11 years old when her sister died and other family trauma followed. She closed off her feelings and communication and had intense anger. She consulted a specialist, but with no resolution. At the age of 21, she had suicidal ideations and started seeing psychiatrists and other counselors for her childhood trauma, daily night-mares, grief, and other emotional issues. Later, she developed other symptoms, including high blood pressure, restless leg syndrome, high cholesterol, and thyroid issues. In previous years, she had several bouts of severe colds and bronchitis, having to use an inhaler. She also suffered from recurring carpal tunnel, shoulder, elbow, knee, and ankle pain and heel spurs. These respiratory issues and joint pains impacted her sense of wellbeing, making it difficult to exercise or even walk.

Acupuncture treatments provided only temporary relief from pain. Medication did help lower her blood pressure. She was prescribed different medicines and received various treatments. She also tried meditation, yoga, tai chi, and numerous other spiritual practices.

In January 2018 she received a blessing and Tao light transmission from Master Sha during Tao Calligraphy Field demonstration session. The same night, she was able to sleep through the night without night terrors for the first time since childhood.

During our research follow-up after one year, she wrote to us that after receiving the blessing and transmission, she experienced reduced craving for sweets, started eating healthier and exercising, and lost nearly ten pounds. She continued to practice Master Sha's techniques for her condition daily. She felt less stress and was sleeping through the nights. She became healthier, stopped having colds, and has not been affected by joint pain.

During our research follow up after two years, she wrote to us that she has continued her daily practices, which include Tao Calligraphy tracing. She was increasing aerobic activity to thirty minutes or more a day and reported feeling more energetic.

Her mental outlook became positive. Her peace of mind has remarkably improved. Before she would constantly worry and would easily become upset or angry. Now, she was able to not become upset or worried, and would become angry with much less frequency and intensity.

Her relationships with her husband and child became more harmonious. Her son was enjoying high school. He was active in music, sports, and clubs, all the while performing well in his academics. Even family pets were enjoying harmony.

After four years of follow-up, she wrote to us this wonderful summary: "My condition has improved. My husband and son (and parents-in-law whom I see weekly) all contracted COVID during the past year, but I have consistently tested negative. My emotions have been balanced. I am able to remain calm and have continued to improve (no colds or respiratory issues since the blessing). I continue my daily practices and invite others to join me. My joints and tendons do not have pain (despite earlier concerns about arthritis). My bone density has tested normal. My blood pressure and other key tests have been in the normal range."

This is such a wonderful healing story on many different levels! We are very happy for her.

Case Study D (a current, ongoing study) in his own words (edited for clarity)

I was diagnosed with depression in my early twenties and have been on medication for depression on and off since that time. After going through a chronic health issue and living in daily pain, I found my depression symptoms getting increasingly worse. I had no energy, I wasn't sleeping at night and found it very difficult to get out of bed most days. I lost interest in nearly everything I used to love. Simple daily tasks, like brushing my teeth and bathing, felt like monumental challenges. I was in a very dark place. Many of the symptoms of my health issues were coming back and I was facing more medical procedures. The medicine I was prescribed was very expensive, which lead to stress and strain in our family finances and on my marriage. All of this escalated the depression to the point that I found myself, for the first time, actually feeling like it might be better for everyone if I were no longer alive.

Thankfully, right at that time this depression study opened and I received a Tao light transmission for healing depression. I practiced with it daily and joined the group practices as often as I could. I cannot even begin to tell you the difference! I feel so much lighter. Better. Like a big dark cloud has transformed and I can feel and see the sunshine again. I have energy to go outside and work in my yard. I feel joy and happiness again. Not to mention my health has greatly improved so that I have not had to resume the very expensive medication! There really are no words that could adequately show the appreciation I have in my heart to have been given this gift of light. I will cherish and use it forever. With deepest gratitude.

Case Study E (a current, ongoing study) in her own words (edited for clarity)

I am currently a college student in college in the USA. I have struggled with anxiety and depression my whole life. However, I was not diagnosed with bipolar depression until I was twenty-one. With bipolar depression I would often feel very imbalanced in my emotions and my mental body. I was hospitalized many times due to this condition and medicated as well. I would often feel so emotional and mentally unbalanced that I could not get through the day. I had to leave school and work so I could heal.

I started doing practices of Dr. and Master Sha daily for one to five hours, received a Tao light transmission for healing depression, and joined the research study for anxiety and depression. In less than a year, my emotions and mental body have transformed. I no longer feel emotionally unstable every day and my mental body feels much more balanced. My heart feels stronger, more capable, and balanced also. These practices and the transmission have changed my life forever.

Thank you, Dr. and Master Sha.

Case Study F (a current, ongoing study) in his own words (edited for clarity and confidentiality)

I am now sixty-six. Years ago, I had an accident that resulted in a broken back in the lumbar section L7 and suffered extreme pain, depression, and anxiety. The trauma was so severe that the first hospital did not have the means to treat me, so the medical team arranged for airvac transport to a trauma center hospital for surgery. After the surgery, I was transferred to a third hospital for twenty-eight days of spinal trauma rehab. From there, my recuperation was maintained in a continuum of care therapy treatment with loving care from my family and relatives. My mother insisted that my doctors approve the continuum of care with my family in our home state.

I will be forever grateful to my bosses (prior to the auto accident, I had three jobs). I can call them my friends, caring people who only wanted my best interests in health and wellbeing. They met my mother and supported her desire to bring me home from the area where I was treated to my family in another state for the long duration of my recovery.

The accident traumatized me. I received medical treatments for the following diagnoses: chronic pain, depression, and anxiety, verifiable by my medical records that were sent to the care of the leader of the study I joined a few years ago, including diagnoses, CT scans, x-rays, and other medical documents confirming my medical condition and documenting the various treatments I received for trauma: pain, depression, and anxiety.

One of my bosses was by my bedside during the first hospital stay and visited me at the second and third hospitals. Another boss and my close friend visited me at two hospitals and agreed with my mother to allow me to return with her to our state to make sure I was taken care of by a doctor who was my good friend. At the second hospital, where I had the surgery, the medical staff told my mother that they had never had a patient who received as many visitors as I had and wanted to know if I was famous. Ha! Just a person who was appreciated and loved by so many friends that left an indelible impression upon me and probably will for the rest of my life. My mother, brother, sister, aunts, uncles, cousins, nieces, and nephews were immensely supportive and provided consolation. My new friends where I was injured and first treated, childhood friends in our state, and my ex-wife and past girlfriends were all supportive and offered prayers and encouragement.

After a long recovery, I returned to the state where I was injured. A friend there noticed how badly I was suffering from anxiety and depression and suggested a book, Feeling Good. He recently told me that the transformation of my mood from anxiety to calmness, was so remarkable that I became his reference story for others on how good the Feeling Good bibliotherapy could be for them. He has a way of caring for people that is unforgettable, and I was of service to others by way of example through his message. He made me feel good, reminding me of an old Dutch proverb: "Pain shared is halved and joy shared is doubled." Nothing in the spiritual universe is lost; the energy exchange between caring souls is healing beyond measure. It was miraculous.

"Miracles occur naturally as expressions of love. The real miracle is the love that inspires them. In this sense, everything that comes from love is a miracle." (A Course in Miracles, p. 83). My mood and spirit were lifted to a noticeable point: an attractive young woman was attracted to me and we fell in love. She accepted my disability unconditionally. What a blessing she was; I thought my love life was over. She is now married to another, so I'll call her Lourdes to protect her confidence. Our relationship lasted two years—as long as with my ex-fiancée. When we ended, I dropped back into a depression and forgot all about Feeling Good. Years passed, and my physical condition *worsened, compounded by anxiety and depression from physical and emotional pain. I isolated and worked as best as I could. My good friend and boss passed away in 2009, my sister and my best friend in the city where I was first treated passed away in 2013, and so did my nutritionist. My mother passed away in 2017. I took all of this to heart and continued to deteriorate physically. I had lapsed back into deep depression and anxiety.*

Although the traditional medical treatment model I received throughout fifteen years was beneficial, I genuinely appreciate being put back together. The road to recovery was arduous and fraught with enduring challenges of pain and suffering and overwhelming depression and anxiety. The help with my medical struggles with my back pain, depression, and anxiety diagnoses was so much appreciated. I had been making recovery progress by the many means received through traditional medicine and alternatives, but I continued to suffer from pain, depression, and anxiety. So, I continued to seek a solution for my painful medical conditions and was introduced to Dr. and Master Sha and his team of healers. I enrolled in Dr. and Master Sha's depression research conducted by the Sha Research Foundation.

Since my enrollment into the Tao Calligraphy Healing research program, I have practiced the calligraphy tracing healing method daily, along with weekly progress check-in and regular monitoring with the study psychologist, who had also monitored my progress periodically with self-administered clinical measuring tools: BDI, PHQ–9, HAM–D, and HAM–A questionnaires. The three-year research study concluded in January

2022. I was one of 600 patients in the research studies that validated my results and that of Dr. and Master Sha's healing methods.

The healing progress since the Tao Calligraphy program with study psychologist has improved my symptoms tremendously in just a short period. Not only was my back pain reduced, but my depression also lifted and my anxiety improved, and other nerve damage-related conditions healed. The unexpected added benefits of the Tao Calligraphy tracing program were that my energy level stabilized, my work performance improved, and I was able to continue pursuit of a doctoral degree in clinical psychology. Last year, the university conferred upon me a second master's degree on the academic journey toward a Ph.D. I completed the necessary course work and am now in the dissertation phase. I did not do these accomplishments alone and believe in possibilities again. As I said, my back pain, depression, and anxiety are so much improved that I can hardly believe it. It's truly a miracle. Try what this book has to offer you and see where it takes you.

For example, before the accident, my career path was well underway, including being an elected official representative of a state-level association for three consecutive two-year terms, the last two of which were Vice President positions. My good friend and I served one of those elected terms together. However, my career was abruptly interrupted by the accident that nearly ended my life and vocation seventeen years ago. My return to the same status and career path was lost to fate and deferred to others that were in line for the elected office. Nothing was ever the same after that traumatic event. My physical and emotional recovery progress was significant. I have so much to be grateful *for my family, friends, colleagues, the medical profession, alternative approaches, self-help spiritual dynamics, and more. However, I was still in depression and struggling with anxiety, and my senior title status was reduced several months before I enrolled in Dr. and Master Sha's Tao Calligraphy research program three years ago. I had to do something, so what led me to seek out Tao Calligraphy as part of my treatment was a lecture I attended by Dr. and Master Sha and his team. The blessings gave me a feeling of hope and restored a sense that a very good possibility for true healing was available.*

Since my enrollment and daily practice in the Tao Calligraphy program with study psychologist and her team weekly follow-up sessions, I had improved progressively throughout the study. My schoolwork improved and I took fewer sick days at my job than I had in years. Before the Tao Calligraphy program, I was calling out sick too often according to my employer. Now that is not an issue raised anymore and I feel much better, with no depression or anxiety. I do not feel ashamed of myself anymore. I have an acceptance and a sense of hope because of Dr. and Master Sha's Tao Calligraphy program with study psychologist and study medical doctor. The additional benefits seem unlimited, such as fellowship with my sponsor. "I know a new freedom and new happiness. I do not regret the past nor wish to shut the door on it. I comprehend the word serenity and know peace." (Big Book of AA, p. 83).

Soul Language fluency (an intuition) continues to evolve. For example, recently, fate brought me to another MD who asked me about one nurse; a few days later, I woke up to the cross I have from her, a gift she gave brought back from Medjugorje divinely inspired to put me back in contact with her and to connect with this doctor again. Other examples: Last year, I became an award-winning author. This year I am nearly done with a third book and was recognized in Who's Who in America (an honor limited to individuals who possess professional integrity, demonstrate outstanding achievement in their respective fields, and have made numerous contributions to society as a whole). By the way, my lead counselor status was returned six months ago. A miracle? Yes, I believe in miracles. Try what this book offers and experience healing from depression and anxiety to wellness and recovery.

This is a truly fascinating story of a professional psychologist whose life was badly damaged from injuries, who suffered for many years, and who eventually, with the support of Dr. and Master Sha's healing system, has fully reclaimed his successful life. We are very happy for him.

༄ ༙ ༚

We are very honored to share these research results and heart-touching stories of our subjects. To be involved in Sha Research Foundation research projects is to have the opportunity to witness, with scientific methods and during interactions with research subjects, the impact of Dr. and Master Sha's techniques. The ability to support these lovely individuals on their path to recovery is very rewarding and uplifting. It is a great privilege that all of us research team members feel deeply in our hearts, and for this we are very grateful. Last year our cancer research team presented a paper at the International Oncology Conference, where they discussed how much positive transformation of their own outlook on life they received from doing this work.

We are also very grateful to all professionals and supportive teams in Sha Research Foundation that have collaborated on our studies over the years. We are immensely grateful to each and every one of hundreds of research subjects who gave their heart and dedication to support our work.

If you would like to review the presentations in more depth or learn more about Sha Research Foundation, please visit www.ShaResearchFoundation.com.

Conclusion

I HAVE A DREAM that humanity will pay more and more attention to self-healing. I honor all medical professionals and all alternative and complementary medicines, as well as all ways to improve our health and happiness.

The message I always share with humanity is:

I have the power to heal myself.
You have the power to heal yourself.
Together we have the power to heal the world.

I have studied Chinese energy and spiritual healing, including tai chi, qi gong, gong fu, *I Ching,* and feng shui, as well as Western medicine and traditional Chinese medicine. I have created Tao Calligraphy.

Through my whole life's study, I have realized in my heart and soul a one-sentence secret for healing and transforming all life:

All challenges in health, relationships, finances, and the spiritual journey are due to negative information, energy, and matter; Tao Calligraphy carries Source most-positive information, energy, and matter, with Source love, light, and frequency, which could transform negative information, energy, and matter in every aspect of life.

This book and subsequent books in the Tao Calligraphy series are bringing the Tao Calligraphy Transformative Art Source Field to humanity to transform every aspect of life.

Recall the ancient secret wisdom: da Dao zhi jian, *the greatest Tao is extremely simple.* The Tao Calligraphy Transformative Art Field is the da Dao zhi jian way to serve humanity in every aspect of life.

It is one of my biggest dreams to serve all humanity. I have created thousands of heart-touching and moving healing results. I do not promise anything. I support all medical and healing systems worldwide. I am a servant for humanity. I am delighted to create the Tao Calligraphy book series to serve.

The Tao Calligraphy Field brings Source power to humanity in order to serve you in every aspect of your life. This is the second book in the Tao Calligraphy series.

Practice. Practice. Practice.
Heal. Heal. Heal.
Transform. Transform. Transform.

I love my heart and soul
I love all humanity
Join hearts and souls together
Love, peace, and harmony
Love, peace, and harmony

Upcoming Books in the Tao Calligraphy Series

UPCOMING VOLUMES WILL focus on:

- Healing the Immune System
- Healing Knee Pain
- Healing Fear
- Healing Shoulder Pain
- Healing Anger
- Healing Heart Issues
- Healing Grief
- Healing the Kidneys
- Healing Worry

In each book of the Tao Calligraphy series, I will write a new and different Tao Calligraphy. I will repeat the key fundamental wisdom and knowledge. I will lead readers to practice in the Tao Calligraphy Field created by one or more Tao Calligraphies in each book.

Made in the USA
Middletown, DE
30 November 2022

16498921R00126